Marva Collins believes that every child is a special creation with the ability to excel. She has proved this, working with children in some of the most poverty-stricken neighborhoods in Chicago.

For those she has taught, the words "I can't" are not in their vocabulary. She teaches that all "can" read, and learn, and compete, and be successful.

She is a remarkable person with a wonderful story to tell, one that can be helpful to all parents of small children.

I admire her greatly and wish that her attitude and example could be replicated in communities across our country.

—Rosalynn Carter

Values

Lighting the Candle of Excellence

A PRACTICAL GUIDE FOR THE FAMILY

by
Marva Collins

DOVE
BOOKS

ISBN: 0-7871-1040-X

Printed in the United States of America

Dove Books
8955 Beverly Boulevard
Los Angeles, CA 90048

Distributed by Penguin USA

Text design and layout by Carolyn Wendt
Jacket design and layout by Rick Penn-Kraus

First Printing: October 1996

10 9 8 7 6 5 4 3 2 1

To Michael Keiser,
whose generosity has made it
possible for thousands of children's eyes
to hold wonder like a cup.

Contents

◆　◆　◆　◆　◆　◆　◆　◆

I Am Excellence

I bear the flame that enlightens the world. I fire the imagination. I give might to the dreams and wings to the aspirations of men.

I create all that is good, stalwart, and long-lasting. I build for the future by making my every effort superior today.

I do not believe in "can't" or "might have been."

When society draws a circle that will shut me out, I will design my own circle that will draw me in.

I am the parent of progress, the creator of creativity, the designer of opportunity, and the molder of human destiny.

Because of me, man holds dominion over himself, his home, his community, and his world. I leash the lightning and plumb the ether.

*From out of the shadows of the past
I come wearing the scars of mistakes
made by others. Yet I wear the wisdom
and the contributions of all ages. I dispel
yesterday's myths and find today's facts.
I am ageless and timeless.*

*I have no time for vice, crime, and
destruction. I banish mediocrity and
discourage being average. I can function
in pleasure or pain. I can steel the will
to do what must be done. Fortunate are
the individuals, communities, and
nations that know me.*

*Men and the world are my workshops.
Here I stir ambition, forge ideals, and create the keys that open the door to worlds
never dreamed of. Earth awakes unfolding
to me. Life is always calling me. My
greatest success is yet to be discovered.*

*I am the source of creation, the outlet of
inspiration, the dream of aspiration. I
am excellence. Won't you, too, light my
candle? Don't let me flicker away!*

Introduction

We are all born with the ability to succeed, to lead a life of excellence. But that ability develops only if it is nurtured. Over the past three decades, I have watched and guided thousands of students in making life choices. I have sought to understand and influence what will help each person find excellence and success. The opportunities we are given in life are often determined by factors beyond our control, but it is what we decide to do with these opportunities that counts. And that is determined by our values.

Values can be taught. Children who are to achieve their dreams need a framework of values they can rely on, reinforced with love and consistency by both parents and teachers. These values are the qualities of character and the modes of thought and feeling we use to find our way through life. They are the guideposts that help us discern what's important to ourselves, our families, and humankind. Without them, a life of excellence is rendered a distant possibility.

My own experiences as a teacher and parent have been informed by the choices I have made, and my successful choices are those in which I was true to myself and to the values I hold dear. I founded the Marva Collins Preparatory Schools with the belief that anything is possible, and the struggles and triumphs of the past twenty years have only fortified that belief.

My odyssey began with my departure from a fourteen-year teaching career in the Chicago public school system. I loved my work and my students, but I knew the system was failing them. Too many students were not learning how to read, were being labeled as failures, and were making disastrous life choices, the first of which was dropping out of school.

I set out to build Westside Preparatory School with $5,000 from my pension fund and the help and support of my family. Together we constructed a classroom space on the second floor of our home. In 1975 my first class consisted of eight students, including two of my own children who I brought over from Chicago's prestigious Francis W. Parker High School. Our voyage had begun.

At first, most of the students at Westside Prep were those who had dropped out, had been expelled, or were failing in the public school system for a variety of reasons. But word spread through the community, and soon our one-room schoolhouse boasted classes of thirty-four children each, with more on the waiting list. An article on our school was published in the *Chicago Sun-Times* and was picked up by wire services. Then *Time* magazine ran a story, and so did *Good Housekeeping, People,* and several educational journals. Local television stations aired segments on us. We had captured the attention of the nation.

What were we doing at Westside Prep? Armed with a rigorous curriculum, nonstop personal caring, and a firm belief in the dignity and self-worth of each and every child, we were out to prove the public school system and the naysayers wrong, that our children *could* succeed in school. Behind our walls, troubled children learned to read and reason, courtesy of Shakespeare, Plato, and Emily Dickinson. Children formerly labeled learning disabled went on to graduate magna cum laude from first-rate universities.

In 1979 the TV news program "60 Minutes"

filmed a segment on Westside Prep. After that show aired, nearly 6,000 letters from interested parents poured in to our office. A made-for-TV movie, *The Marva Collins Story,* starring Cicely Tyson, was produced. With money from this endeavor and from private contributions, we were able to move the school out of our home and into two renovated factory buildings. Today, Westside Prep and two Marva Collins Preparatory schools exist (one in Chicago and one in Cincinnati), and over the past twenty-one years they have graduated 13,000 students.

Extracurricular programs at our schools include the Mentally Gifted Forum. Children attend the forum on a volunteer basis to study the works of Lao-Tzu, Buddha, Friedrich Nietzsche, Fyodor Dostoyevsky, and Plato, among others. On weekends, students are invited to come and participate in literary discussions, science fairs, and vocabulary contests. Parents often attend, too.

Our schools accept no federal funds or corporate grants. They are funded through student tuition and through the lectures and training seminars I conduct across the country. I have trained approximately 30,000 teachers, principals, and administrators from all over the world.

Once, during a training session at Westside Prep, the children were trying my patience, as children will. They had decided to act a bit unruly in front of two hundred or so teachers who were attending the session. I said to them calmly, "If I hear further noise, I will leave the room. I will never give you more homework, and I will never hold this class again."

Complete silence. The visiting teachers could not believe it. Later they told me, "Had they been my students, they would have broken out in applause."

One of the greatest accolades I have ever received came from an eleven-year-old boy who wrote me the following letter:

Dear Mrs. Collins,

Throughout the years I have known you, your warm and gentle words have always brightened my dark days. My love for you is everlasting. Whenever I feel blue or doubtful, I think of you. I think of your kind words, your determination to see all children succeed, your caring eyes. You have given me and so many other children a bond that separates us from the average people in the world. You always taught us that average people are never in short supply, and so thank you for the journey into the land of excellence.

Love,
Jason Swan

One day two of my students had an altercation on the bus. Rather than punishing them, I wrote the following words. They became the creed of Westside Preparatory School. The children say it every morning, and whenever they are in trouble, they must repeat a line from the creed that is appropriate to their problem. Here is just a portion of it:

I will use each day to the fullest. I promise that each day shall be gained, not lost—used, not thrown away. Yet, it is my privilege to destroy myself if that is what I choose to do.

I have the right to fail, but I do not have the right to take my teacher and other people with me. God made me the captain of only one life...my own....

Without education, what is man?
A splendid slave, a savage, a beast
wandering from here to there believing
whatever he is told....

God is not some cosmic bellboy that
comes at my beck and call. If I want
to achieve, the first step must be my
undertaking....

I can swiftly stand up and shout:
"This is my time and place, I will
accept the challenge!"

Values: Lighting the Candle of Excellence highlights thirty principles or qualities in alphabetical order, supplemented with practical tips and "Try this" exercises on how to explain and teach these concepts to your children. I have also included personal stories of how these methods have worked in my own family. It is not necessary to read this book in a linear fashion. Read the sections that interest you most first, then go back and focus on the others—you never know what you might be missing. Share this book with your spouse or partner, your relatives, and your children.

You are the best judge of when your child is ready to learn. But never forget: Every child is teachable, and it is never too early to start on the road of education.

As a parent, you are your child's first teacher, and your home is your child's first school. Whether it is creativity, family, kindness and compassion, self-reliance, thinking, or any of the other core values that we wish to impart to our children, I hope you will have, after reading this book, a wealth of new ideas and techniques you can use to establish that important framework of values your child needs.

Once excellence becomes a habit with children, we see it manifest in everything they do. They become self-motivated. They have more confidence. They set goals for themselves. Talk with your children. Nurture their ways of thinking and growing. It is an investment not only in your children's future but also in our economy, our communities, our very survival.

Affirmation

*I am a special child, I am worth
celebrating, today I celebrate me.*
—Marva Collins

Most of us would never dream of with-
holding food from our children for days
at a time, for a week, or even for a month. The
very idea is deplorable and unthinkable. Yet
how many days, weeks, months go by without
positive parental affirmation? I remember writing a special note every night to each of my
three children and putting these messages of
love at their breakfast places.

In our issue-a-week society and our hurry-up
world, it is easy to forget our first priority...our
children. If we can get the child together, we
surely will have the world together.

Just as we prioritize our activities at work
and at home—from business meetings to doing
the laundry—*we must remember to find time
each day, every day, to affirm our love for our*

children. Buying a new pair of sneakers, the hottest new outfit, or an expensive trinket, however, does not assure your child of your love. Only *you* can do that. Material things can never take the place of love and security. When your child is asked, "What do you know for sure?" and can say with certainty, "I know for sure my parents love me," he or she is ready to encounter almost any of life's difficulties.

When was the last time you made deposits into your child's emotional and physical "bank account"? Is your child overdrawn? In the morning, try saying: "Good morning, I am so glad you are being cooperative today." If your child is dawdling while you are rushing to get to work, say: "You know, I really depend on your cooperation to get to work on time. I would like it so very much if you could make the morning a really good one."

◆ ◆

TRY THIS
Daily Deposits

Write a series of notes for your child. They might say: "You are a winner! I am so glad you are a part of our family," or "I love you so very much," or "Thank you for all the help you give us/me," or "Have a great day because you are a great boy/girl," or "Ten Reasons Why I Love You," followed by a list of the reasons. Place these notes in your child's lunch pail, on your child's pillow at night, on your child's dresser, in your child's coat pocket, and so forth.

What we begin, however, we must continue. Remember that information not caught has not been thoroughly taught. *Consistency and repetition are the key.* Every deposit you make with your child provides armor against the cruelties and the wrong hands that beckon in the real world. Your child can never become overdrawn if you make the right deposits daily.

◆ ◆

NOTES

_____

_____

_____

Beliefs

As a man or woman thinketh,
so are they.
                    —Proverbs 23:7

*O*nly as far as I see can I go, only as much as I dream can I be, only as high as I reach can I grasp. Our beliefs are akin to a permanent road map: They define our territory and help us navigate the various paths within it. If we believe there is only one way to do something, we will be imprisoned by that one way. However, if our belief system tells us, "Maybe others think there is only one way to do something, but I believe I can find many ways to do the same chore, or the same endeavor," we can go far.

I often ask children: If I have 6,000 pieces of Legos, and they have 100 pieces of Legos, which of us will be able to make the most designs and patterns? They think right away that, of course, I will. Is it because I am more intelligent, or is it because of the color of my skin, or is it because fortune favors me? Of course not. It is only because I have more Legos with which to work. So it is in life. The more materials we have, the more designs we are going to be able to create.

Parents, teachers, and caregivers are the first molders of a child's belief system. Everything we say and do is "recorded" on a "tape" that becomes a part of our children's belief system. And remember, children will do more of what they see us do than of what they hear us say. Think of your actions, your words, and your beliefs as you contribute to this tape. How you solve problems, how you and your spouse or partner respond to each other, how family members communicate—everything counts. And your "recorder" is always on. You are always taping lessons for your child. This recorder allows for no erasures.

What you tape is what your child will hear and live. If you want your child to be fair, you must practice fairness in all of your dealings. If you want your child to be loving, you must show love. If you want your child to enjoy reading, you must read. If you want your child to be calm, you must exhibit calmness. If you want your child to show patience, you must be patient as well. Record brilliantly, or be forced to hear your own negative tape played back by your child in later years.

If a child hears only great concertos and great classical music and is never exposed to any other kind of music, what do we suppose our children will likely choose to listen to as they mature? Right. They will choose what they hear. They will repeat what we record. They will think in the way we and other caregivers have taught them to think. *Teach your child to think lofty, majestic, laudable thoughts.* Record wonderful messages that will lead your child to become an Olympic champion who will stand in the winning circle of life.

Without the right belief systems, children can often become lost on the journey of life. There are so many truths calling to our children that it can be difficult for them to determine which truths are right for them. There are historic truths, parental truths, societal truths, and peer truths, to name just a few. Many children end up abusing drugs or alcohol or acting out in school because they are following peer truths.

We will reach our final destinations only if

we have a clear view of where we would like to go. Likewise, without a road map, our children's successful voyage in life becomes solely a result of luck. Ask yourself: "Where do I want my child to go?" and "What am I willing to do to give my child the ability to reach his or her final destination?"

◆　◆　◆　◆　◆　◆　◆　◆　◆　◆　◆　◆　◆　◆　◆　◆　◆　◆　◆　◆

TRY THIS
The Story of the Little Engine That Could

The classic book *The Little Engine That Could* is a great tool for teaching the importance of believing in oneself. The story tells of a little engine who met with nothing but rejection from the other trains, who were all too busy to help him push the big train. Then he had a thought: He could do the job if he just put his mind to it. The little engine put his shoulder to the train and pushed...and pushed...and pushed, telling himself all the while, "I think I can, I think I can." Soon he discovered that he could do all along what he had thought others had to do for him.

When your child appears to be developing the belief system of "I can't," remind him or her of the Little Engine That Could.

♦ ♦

NOTES

_____

_____

_____

_____

_____

_____

_____

_____

_____

_____

_____

_____

Choice

*We become what we are
by the choices we make.*
     —Marva Collins

I often think of the many confrontations I have seen between parents and children as I travel throughout the country, and I recall an incident with my own four-year-old grandson, Sean, who, as most four-year-olds do, says the word no as if by instinct. One day we were out shopping, and when it was time to leave, Sean backed into a corner and defiantly said, "No, I am not going!" I reached into my purse, took out a dollar bill, and said gently, "Sweetheart, here is a dollar. Take the bus home, and be sure to call me when you get there."

Being a student at our school, Sean thought for a moment. I turned and walked away. Soon I heard footsteps behind me. He rapidly caught up with me and said, "Grandma, I made the wrong choice. I am going home with you."

I hugged him and said, "I am so proud of you. You always make such good choices."

Children will make good decisions based only on the number of patterns with which we have given them to work. If we purchased a pattern with which to make a dress or suit, what would happen if some of the pieces were missing? Either we would resort to alternative thinking or we would be at a loss to complete the design in mind.

Negative punishment gives our children negative patterns with which they will ultimately always come up with the wrong answers. If we hear enough wrong answers in life, we soon decide that we are just plain no good. This is a self-defeating conclusion because there is nothing wrong with us, there is only something wrong with the kind of pattern we have been given. The carpenters of our life measured wrong, cut wrong, and did not bother making us "stick." Every positive punishment we give our children brings home the idea that we love our children without question, we validate them, and we are unhappy only about their negative behavior.

For Every Action...There Is a Reaction

My daughter-in-law, Cheryl, is a teacher at one of our schools, and I am lucky that my grandchildren are taught with the same methodology used at our schools. Ever since the grandchildren were born, one day a week is our time alone. I remember one Sunday afternoon when Cheryl was preparing to bring them to Grandma's. Five-year-old Sean could not make up his mind as to which shirt he wanted to wear. Cheryl said to him: "Sean, since you can't make up your mind, you must suffer the consequences and stay home with Mom and Dad today." His sister, little Bri, excitedly burst into our home with the following message: "Grandma, Grandma, Sean couldn't come to your house today, he made the wrong choice and he must suffer the quences." The word *consequences* did not quite make it out of her young mouth, but she had the idea.

When children say to you, "I will not do that," rather than argue with them, agree with them. Simply say: "I think that is a wonderful idea, but now let's consider the consequences of your choices." You are now leading the child to discover that every choice has a consequence.

When we think these consequences out before we act, we learn to "proofread" life the way we would proofread a paper we have written. By plucking out bad thinking before an act takes place, we will have fewer errors by the end of the act.

While waiting to board a plane one day, I heard a parent tell her five-year-old at least twenty times not to put his fingers in the heavy door that led out to the plane. After hearing the child's resounding no's more than I could bear, I finally left my seat and walked over. "Hello, Jason," I said. (And how could I *not* know his name, having heard his mom repeat it several times!) "My name is Mrs. Collins. And Jason, it's really okay if you want to put your fingers in the door. You see, I happen to know the people who work here at the airport and they have been looking for a little boy or girl who is willing to give up a finger; you see, they need another button for the door, and the only way they can get a new button is to have someone give up a finger. Shall I tell them I have found someone willing to give up a finger so they can get the button they need?"

Jason didn't answer. I continued, "Of course, you have the right to put your fingers in the door, but the consequences will be that you will be missing one finger. Now shall I go and tell them I have found someone?"

Jason looked up at me with frightened eyes and replied, "No, ma'am, I don't want to put my fingers in the door anymore."

I hugged him and said, "You are so bright. You have made a wonderful choice. I wouldn't want to lose one of my fingers either."

His grateful mother said to me with a smile, "Would you like to come home with us?"

One simple conversation with Jason was all that was needed to change his behavior, and the choice was his, not mine. *Teaching our children about making the right choices is perhaps the very best thing we can ever do for them.* Later on, when their peers try to persuade them to make wrong choices, our children will remember that every choice has a consequence.

♦ ♦

TRY THIS
Cause and Effect

Read the following popular Mother Goose rhyme with your child.

Little Boy Blue, come blow your horn,
The sheep are in the meadow,
The cows are in the corn.
Where's the little boy who tends the sheep?
He's under the haystack fast asleep.

Discuss the meaning of the word *tend* (to keep or look after) with your youngster. Ask which line reveals that Little Boy Blue is not very dependable. Teach the concept of cause and effect by pointing out the following: Little Boy Blue fell asleep while working, and now the sheep have strayed to the meadow and the cows are eating the farmer's corn. The farmer will have no corn to sell at the market, and as a result people will have no corn to eat. The farmer cannot pay his bills if he has no corn to sell. When we are not acting responsibly, bad things can happen that may affect many people.

* *

NOTES

_____

_____

Confidence

Trust thyself. Every heart vibrates to that iron string.
—Ralph Waldo Emerson

Confidence is not something we can simply purchase on our American Express or Visa cards. *Confidence is something we achieve with repetition and by building self-esteem. Amazingly enough, it comes to us through the challenges that are truly difficult rather than through those that are easy.* Once we tackle enough challenges and find that we have come out whole, we are then ready to take on other, perhaps more difficult, challenges.

Confidence begins as soon as children can walk and talk. We must say to our children: "If you can't do it, I will be here to help, but first you must try." This means, for example, watching them struggle to tie their shoelaces, to walk up and down the stairs, to feed themselves, to dress themselves. Don't worry if the heels of the socks end up at the tops of their feet the first time. It is easier for you, the parent, to do it for them, but children learn by doing things on their own. They learn perhaps even more from what they do *not* do correctly.

The Importance of "I Can"

Words are very powerful. Remember, young children come to us with a blank tape. If you have already recorded for them words such as *can't* and *can,* they will learn to associate these words with tasks they attempt to accomplish. Therefore, rather than saying to your child, "I think you can't do that," a more appropriate question might be: "Are you sure you have considered all the facts before attempting that?" "Have you thought of other ways this might be done?" or "I like the way you tied your shoes, but can you think of other ways you could do it?"

Children who grow up thinking "I can" will never accept "You can't." Whenever we ask our three- and four-year-olds at Westside Preparatory School how they know this or that, the reply is always: "Because I am bright. I can do anything." *If a child thinks he or she can do anything, there is nothing anyone can do to sap that child's self-esteem or confidence.*

The more alternative modes of thinking you give your children, the better they are going to do academically and socially in the journey of life. The more love, praise, and confidence we give our children, the more they will evolve into self-assured individuals. Children who are truly confident will grow up not depending on others for validation of their decisions and feelings. If you record and give your children their own positive tape (see Beliefs), you will allow them to automatically tune in and listen to it when they hear negative tapes from others.

The standardized tests your child takes in school are considered, in large part, tests of ability. They measure knowledge gained or learned, as well as thinking ability, vocabulary, and comparison and contrast skills. It's important to remember there is a real difference between *what* a child learns and the *capacity* of that child to learn. Rarely will your child be graded or scored on capacity. If your child enters school with great confidence and basic critical and analytical thinking skills, he or she is already prepared never to accept failure and tracking. *You, the parent, must begin early to prepare your child so that no teacher or school will ever be able to allow him or her to establish a habit of failing, or to be tracked as being "slow."*

Life Is Like Riding a Bicycle

How many of us can remember that first bicycle ride? I was about seven years old when I received a wonderful red-and-white bicycle for Christmas. Of course, having a great deal of confidence in myself, I assumed that riding a bicycle was just another of life's tasks, something I would surely be able to accomplish. So I set out to ride that bicycle, never once thinking that it was beyond my abilities.

My father insisted that he help balance me, and of course I retorted: "I can do it…I can do it all by myself." Off I went. The next thing I knew, I had crashed into a large telegraph post and was forced to spend the rest of the day in bed with skinned legs.

To learn to ride a bicycle, one needs more than a will. One also needs balance and know-how. Life is pretty much like that bicycle. We all need balance, know-how, and a sense of confidence. Life can become wobbly at times, and sometimes we may fall, but we should never let one fall deter us from getting on that bicycle again.

The following poem by William Ernest Henley helps illustrate the bicycle metaphor.

Invictus

Out of the night covers me
Black as the Pit from pole to pole
I thank whatever gods may be
For my unconquerable soul.

In the fell clutch of circumstance
I have not winced nor cried aloud.
Under the bludgeoning of chance
My head is bloody, but unbowed.

Beyond the place of wrath and tears
Looms but the horror of the shade,

And yet the menace of the years,
Finds and shall find me unafraid.

It matters not how strait the gate,
How charged with punishment
*   the scroll,*
I am the captain of my fate,
I am the master of my soul.

◆ ◆ ◆ ◆ ◆ ◆ ◆ ◆ ◆ ◆ ◆ ◆ ◆ ◆ ◆ ◆ ◆ ◆ ◆ ◆

TRY THIS

Everyday Learning

Learning is everywhere. You can prepare your child for standardized school tests by encouraging them to learn about the world around them. While grocery shopping, say to your child: "These are apples. Do they grow on a tree or a vine?" "These are onions. Do they grow on a tree, a vine, or in the ground?" Talk to your child frequently and in clear detail: "Bring me the blue dish on the second shelf," or "Bring me the red bowl to the left of the green bowl." *Children who learn to listen carefully to directions will do well in school.*

♦ ♦

NOTES

_____

_____

_____

_____

_____

_____

_____

_____

_____

_____

_____

Creativity

Human salvation lies in the hands of
the creatively maladjusted.
—the Rev. Martin Luther King, Jr.

*C*reativity *is parallel thinking. It is seeing new ways, new models, new alternatives to doing something.* I often buy colorful kites to display inside my home. More than once I have been instructed by the salesperson how to fly the kites after I assemble them. She or he is always amused when I reply, "But I do not plan to fly the kite. I'm going to put it on my wall at home." Likewise, I often purchase colorful shawls that many women would wear around their shoulders, but instead my shawls often become tablecloths, couch covers, or bed covers, and yes, sometimes I may wear one as a shawl. This is creativity.

The story of scientist and mathematician Sir Isaac Newton, who is believed to have discovered the law of gravity, is a typical one of creativity and parallel thinking. When he reportedly saw the apple fall, he did not say: "That stupid apple fell." Instead, he wondered: "Why did the apple fall this way? Why didn't it fall another way?" He kept wondering until he realized that the apple fell because of gravitational pull.

◆ ◆

TRY THIS
Infinite Creativity

Creativity is taking a sheet of paper and constructing shapes, designs, and figures from what others may see as just a sheet of paper. Having children create forms using old buttons, beads, scraps of fabric, popsicle sticks, jewelry, paper clips, dried pasta shapes, and so forth is a wonderful way to help them express their creativity. For example, have them glue together popsicle sticks to make a photo frame, then decorate it by gluing on beads, glitter, shapes cut out of fabric, old brooches, and dried macaroni. The possibilities are endless.

◆ ◆

Creativity is leaping ahead with a vision and then looking back later to uncover why it happened and what steps were taken to get there. The more a child learns to create, the greater his or her confidence becomes. If we teach our children to ask why, when, and where, we will help them find alternative ways of doing what others have often declared impossible.

Food for Thought

Set aside some time at the dinner table to discuss ideas. You may call this Idea Time. Each family member will be responsible for presenting a new idea. During this time, children should be taught the virtue of listening, thinking, and evaluating before responding. Encourage them to respect each other's differences. Emphasize that there should be no ridiculing of any family member. *Every idea deserves attention.*

Use the word *idea* in everyday conversation. When solving a problem, say, "I have an idea," and state your idea. Then ask your child, "What do you think? Do you have an idea?"

Idea has become an ordinary word in the Collins family. When I make a bad decision, my three-year-old granddaughter, Bri, will say, "Bad idea, Grandma." We often play the good idea, bad idea game using values I or their parents are trying to teach them. For example, I will say, "All Collinses are failures," or "Let's cross the street without looking both ways." One of my grandchildren will respond, "Bad idea, Grandma."

We often attempt to teach our children values without reinforcement. Just as Madison Avenue drills ideas into our children about what they want for holiday presents, we parents must repeat again and again the values we would like our children to remember.

NOTES

_____

_____

_____

_____

Direction

Concentrate, and you will radiate.
—Marva Collins

Would we normally get into our cars and drive off without knowing what direction we were headed in? What would happen if we stopped to shop? If we stopped to admire the scenery? If we stopped to talk to a neighbor? If we stopped at the library or the bank?

The word *mission* means to set a goal, to know where we are headed and how we're going to get there. I highly recommend you and your family create individual mission statements. It is the best way I know of to bring yourselves together as a unit and form a strong foundation with which you can best define family values and inspire excellence.

First, explain the meaning of the word *mission* to your family and children. Make certain the entire family, adults and all children, understands the meaning and why a mission statement is so important.

You are now ready to write your mission statements. Very young children who cannot yet write may dictate their mission statement to an older sibling, or you, the parent, may write it for them.

A parent's mission statement might read as follows: "As the mother of this family, it is my mission to always be an example of excellence for my children and my husband so that I become what I would like them to be. I will at all times practice the excellent team spirit that I wish from my family. I will learn to listen as well as speak, to forgive as well as criticize, and to provide a nourishing, loving, and comfortable place for me and my family. That is my mission."

Here is an example of a child's mission statement: "As a member of this family, I will work each day to become an effective team member. As a part of that, I will take the garbage out every other day. I will help my younger sister with her homework when she asks me. I will pursue excellence in everything that I do. I realize that excellence is a lifetime habit and not a daily act."

Every member of the family should prepare and write her or his own mission statement. You might want to include statements from baby-sitters and other caregivers as well. Each mission statement should be hung in the family room or some other favorite place in the home. They may be framed and can be handed down to future generations.

♦ ♦

TRY THIS
The Family Mission Statement

Family members should collaborate on one mission statement that the entire family can adhere to. This statement will remind each person of their lifetime mission. Daily disagreements will therefore become less important when the family can consider the lifetime commitment they have made together.

♦ ♦

NOTES

_____

_____

_____

_____

_____

_____

_____

_____

_____

_____

_____

_____

_____

_____

Discipline and Perseverance

There is no chance, no destiny, no fate
Can circumvent or hinder or control
The firm resolve of a determined soul.
 —from the poem "Solitude"
 by Ella Wheeler Wilcox

The most difficult job of parenting and teaching is to be what we want our children to be, and to do what we would like our children to do. This means practicing discipline. If we were disciplined, we wouldn't smoke, we wouldn't drink too much, we wouldn't overeat, and we would never do the things we should not do. Not many of us fit this category, and thus our children do as we do, not as we say.

If our children hear us say, "This is hard but not impossible" or "I will persevere until I succeed" instead of "I can't take any more of this," they will parrot these words.

Poetry and proverbs can do wonders to create the images in our children that we as parents would love to see. This little poem is an ideal affirmation to repeat to our children: "Somebody said it couldn't be done / But with a chuckle and a grin / I tackled the thing that somebody said couldn't be done / And I did it." At Westside Prep, whenever a student uses the word *can't,* a teacher asks, "What do you need to tell yourself right now?" The child replies, "I need to remove the 't' from the word *can't.*" To which the teacher says, "You are so bright, I knew you could do it."

"Once a task has begun, never leave it until it's done, though the task be great or small, do it well or not at all," is a proverb repeated often by our three- and four-year-old students. When a student attempts to give a teacher a paper that is less than excellent, the teacher asks, "Bright one, what do you need to tell me right now?" The child answers, "This task is not done well at all." The child has done a personal evaluation of his or her own work. What a wonderful lifetime skill!

◆ ◆

TRY THIS
Reading the Odyssey

I cannot think of a greater work than Homer's *Odyssey* to teach children patience, determination, stick-to-it-iveness, and the ability to think. The classic epic chronicles the journey home of Odysseus after he helped Greece defeat Troy in the Trojan War. Can you imagine the perseverance of a warrior who travels ten long years to return home? Can you imagine the cleverness of Odysseus after all the other ships crashed into the rocks because the men aboard became so enchanted with the sweet songs of the siren Circe? He told his own men to plug their ears, thereby safely avoiding the siren's beckon. What a wonderful lesson to teach our children, especially in a world in which far too many of them tell us they did something because "everyone else was doing it." The *Odyssey* and the *Iliad,* which tells the story of the Trojan War, can be read in portions as a family during Family Hour or Sharing Time (see Family).

◆ ◆

The following passage, from Book IX of Homer's *Odyssey*, illustrates the courage and persistence of Odysseus as he journeys home after the Trojan War.

From there we sailed on further along,
*   glad to have escaped death,*
but grieving still at heart for the loss of
*   our dear companions.*
Even then I would not suffer the flight of
*   my oarswept vessels*
until a cry had been made three times
*   for each of my wretched*
companions, who died there in the
*   plain, killed by the Kikonians.*
Cloud-gathering Zeus drove the North
*   Wind against our vessels*
in a supernatural storm, and huddled
*   under the cloud scuds*
land alike and the great water. Night
*   sprang from heaven.*
The ships were swept along yawing
*   down the current; the violence*
of the wind ripped our sails into three
*   and four pieces. These then,*

in fear of destruction, we took down
  and stowed in the ships' hulls,
and rowed them on ourselves until we
  had made the mainland.
There for two nights and two days
  together we lay up,
for pain and weariness together eating
  our hearts out.
But when the fair-haired Dawn in her
  rounds brought on the third day,
we, setting the masts upright, and hoist-
  ing the white sails on them,
sat still, and let the wind and the steers-
  men hold them steady.
And now I would have come home
  unscathed to the land of my fathers,
but as I turned the hook of Maleia, the
  sea and current
and the North Wind beat me off course,
  and drove me on past Kythera.
 Nine days then I was swept along by
  the force of the hostile
winds on the fishy sea, but on the tenth
  day we landed
in the country of the Lotus-Eaters, who
  live on a flowering
food, and there we set foot on the

mainland, and fetched water,
and my companions soon took their
supper there by the fast ships.
But after we had tasted of food and
drink, then I sent
some of my companions ahead, telling
them to find out
what men, eaters of bread, might live
here in this country.
I chose two men, and sent a third with
them, as a herald.
My men went on and presently met the
Lotus-Eaters,
nor did these Lotus-Eaters have any
thoughts of destroying
our companions, but they only gave
them lotus to taste of.
But any of them who ate the honey-
sweet fruit of lotus
was unwilling to take any message
back, or to go
away, but they wanted to stay there with
the lotus-eating
people, feeding on lotus, and forget the
way home. I myself
took these men back weeping, by force,
to where the ships were,

*and put them aboard under the rowing
    benches and tied them
fast, then gave the order to the rest of
    my eager
companions to embark on the ships in
    haste, for fear
someone else might taste of the lotus
    and forget the way home,
and the men quickly went aboard and
    sat to the oarlocks,
and sitting well in order dashed the
    oars in the gray sea.*

NOTES

_____

_____

_____

_____

_____

Do It Now

Putting off tough jobs makes them harder.
—Marva Collins

How many adults do you know who procrastinate and put off for the future what they could do today? I know quite a few, including myself sometimes. If we continuously make excuses and put off things, our children, too, will learn to do the same.

Be a role model to your children. If you need to take the car to the mechanic, write a letter to your aunt Sylvia, or weed the front lawn, do it now. Make taking action right away a habit. By doing so, you present a consistent image of the Do-It-Now habit to your children. The more you insist on the "now" for yourself and your family, the sooner children will develop the habit of not putting off the "now" for the "later."

Nothing hits home like the lesson of promising to take children to their special recreational places, or a special movie on weekends, then saying to them as the time approaches: "Why don't we do that later; maybe next weekend?" Children then learn that the crew and the captain alike can both say: "I forgot, I'll do it later." Once they learn the lesson of "later versus now," they will have learned one of the most important lessons of their lives.

◆ ◆

TRY THIS
Making Learning Count

When children are old enough to read simple books, take a book and have your child count the total number of pages. Then ask, "How many pages must you read per day in order to have finished the book in one week? In two weeks?" Encourage your child to start the book and reach the goal. Make certain he or she does not skip a day's reading; explain to your youngster that if we skip a certain number of pages on one day, we must double the number of pages read the next day if we are to meet our deadline.

◆ ◆

Share the following anonymous poem with your child.

Mr. Meant-To

Mr. Meant-To has a friend, his name is
        Didn't Do
Have you met them?
Did they ever call upon you?
They live together in a house called
        Never Win
And I am told that it is haunted by the
        Ghost of Might Have Been.

If your child fails to accomplish a task and starts to procrastinate on subsequent tasks, ask gently, "Are you becoming a Ms. Meant-To, or a Mr. Meant-To? Remember, they lived in a house called Never Win. Do you want that to happen to you? Bright one, you don't want to end up being a Might Have Been, do you?"

NOTES

Dreams

Dreams are necessary to life.
                                    —Anaïs Nin

Dreams are thought of as feats that others consider impossible. But in reality, many of the luxuries and potentials we enjoy today are the results of someone's dream, someone's thoughts that were put into action.

A low-priced automobile for the masses? Impossible, said many, but Henry Ford made the impossible possible. Pasteurization of food? Impossible again, roared the cynics. But today we all benefit from pasteurized milk. Surgery without pain? Madness, cried the cynics once more. But today those of us who must undergo surgery can thank the person who developed anesthesia.

Our children must be taught to hold fast to their dreams, to believe that their dreams, too, can come to fruition, but only if they are willing to work to make them a reality. Dreams that we are not willing to make happen become pipe dreams, things we mean to get around to one day. By all means, dream, aspire, but do not ruin the life you lead by letting unfulfilled dreams become your master. Rattling around is too big a job.

Before we can get children to do anything, we must always make certain that they see us as adult role models. For example, do we follow our own dreams? Or do we simply call them "wants" and never do anything to make them a reality?

. . . .

TRY THIS
Dear Diary

Encourage your child to keep a diary called *My Dreams.* Ask each week or every other week, "How are we coming on those dreams, bright one?" If the child gives a negative answer, ask, "What are you doing right now to make your dreams come true? What are you willing to do to make your dreams come true?"

. . . .

The poem "Dreams" by Langston Hughes is a marvelous one to hang in your child's room. You might want to write it in calligraphy on poster-size paper and give it to your child as a birthday or holiday present.

Dreams

Hold fast to dreams
For if dreams die
Life is a broken-winged bird
That cannot fly.

Hold fast to dreams
For if dreams go
Life is a barren field
Frozen with snow.

NOTES

Excellence

Excellence is not an act but a habit.
                                    —Aristotle

We often expect praise for a job well done. This is wonderful and encouraging if it happens, but we must teach our children that *excellence is its own reward.* Excellence builds our self-esteem. It is our light in a dark world. It is our teacher when all of our teachers are no longer around. It is our parent when our parents are no longer with us. It is the sole motivator that distinguishes the winners from the losers in life.

Excellence as a daily habit becomes a lifetime solace. We hear a lot about boredom today because we have failed to teach our children the pursuit of excellence. When we do things well for ourselves and not for the praise it will bring, we learn to like ourselves, we learn to like others, and we learn to like our world. When children experience this satisfying feeling, they become addicted to being excellent all the time.

When something is not done well, don't preach to your child. Instead, ask: "Mary, what do you need to tell me about the work you have just completed?" Teach your child to say: "Mother, I think I need to tell you that what I have just done is not excellent, and I am just too bright not to have done it in a more excellent way." Consistency in and repetition of this practice will become a permanent part of your child's behavior.

Try to praise your child daily for random acts of excellence. Even everyday things deserve recognition. For instance, tell your child you are proud of her or him for being a helpful brother or sister, for being a good listener, for finishing that big project, and so on.

My grandson, Sean, has discovered that when he reads difficult signs in hearing range of other people, he gets all kinds of accolades and questions. We were at a department store one day, and he saw a sign that read: EMPLOYEE ENTRANCE ONLY. He read the sign out loud. At age four, this was quite a feat. People around us started asking: "Where does he go to school?"

"How did he learn to read so early?" All had seen Sean's eyes holding wonder like a cup. He later told me: "I get attention because I am so bright."

The following poem makes a great affirmation to hang on the wall. Insert your family surname in the blank.

The _____ family is a miracle
There is nothing that together we
    cannot do.
We work, play, and strive for success
    as a team.
We believe that success is more than
    just a dream.
And so, each day we all contribute
To life's wonderful exhibit
And knowing that anything can be
If only we allow excellence to be free
And to know that progress begins
    not with you, but with me.

• •

TRY THIS
A Schedule of Excellence

Get your children in the habit of making a schedule for excellence at home and at school. This will help your child build pride in his or her accomplishments and help you keep track of them. The schedule may look like this:

My Schedule of Excellence

by _____

DATE	TASK PERFORMED (HOME)	TASK PERFORMED (SCHOOL)
Monday	straightened my room	took my spelling test
Tuesday	helped my brother with homework	read my book report aloud
Wednesday		
Thursday		
Friday		
Saturday		
Sunday		

• •

NOTES

Family

*The family that talks together
stays together.*
—Marva Collins

I think of family as parts of an extension cord used to make a good connection. If we do not connect, we as a family unit can never know brightness and joy in our lives.

Families cannot be ordered, nor can they be put on a payment plan. Unlike products, we are all stuck with the family given us, and they cannot be returned. Most of us feel that our own families are unique, that there is surely no one else in the world like them. Many of us feel embarrassed by some of the antics of our family members. If we could talk to all families, however, we would find that families are more alike than different. *Successful families are those who work to resolve what is not a good family, and therefore what is left is a good family.* If we carve away all the bad things about our families, we have only the good remaining.

How many of us actually plan for good families? How many of us put aside time in our day runners for family? We seem to find time for everything except our families.

My husband and I and our three children found time one day a week to have what we called a Lemon Squeeze. During this session, every family member could tell the others what he or she liked or disliked most about our family. This tactic often produced tears and disagreements, but at least we were talking and listening to one another. And if we continued a dialogue long enough, we did find solutions.

I never tossed out the Mother's Day gifts that my young children gave me. Many of these were simply objects from a penny gumball machine or a cup made at school. I keep them in a special cabinet where each adult child can see her or his initial benevolent attempts. It brings laughter to them and reminds them of how much they've grown. A special gift I gave to my oldest son, Eric, was a framed copy of his first paper, which he wrote when he was five years old. When his son, Sean, began school, I framed one of his first papers. On Father's Day I gave them both to Eric. Now Sean can see that his father, too, once sat at a school desk laboring over schoolwork, and Eric, in turn, can see the similarity between his and Sean's handwriting.

Families are special. These days, we hear so much about the breakdown of family values, I feel that it's time to put family first. After all, if we lose our families, all of our other successes will not matter. To me, the most successful people in the world are those who not only are successful in their chosen goals, but who also brought their families along with them.

There are no free rides when it comes to nurturing strong family relationships. Either we pay now in terms of time spent with our families, or we are left with deep regrets of what might have been.

Many adults find it easier to criticize than to give praise. To help prevent your children from doing the same, accentuate the positive. Every Thanksgiving, each child and adult in my family stands up and tells what he or she is most thankful for, and what he or she plans to do within the next year to make the family stronger. We do the same at Christmas and on New Year's Day. In your family, you might want to suggest that before each family member retires for the night, she or he can say to each of the others, "I am glad you are a part of our family because..."

♦ ♦ ♦ ♦ ♦ ♦ ♦ ♦ ♦ ♦ ♦ ♦ ♦ ♦ ♦ ♦ ♦ ♦ ♦ ♦

TRY THIS
A Homemade Family Heirloom

Here's a fun way to create a family keepsake. On a white tablecloth, have each family member sign her or his name each year. Then, choose one member to be responsible for embroidering over the written names. Younger family members may need help in writing their names. In years to come, they can look back in amusement at the evolution of their signatures.

♦ ♦ ♦ ♦ ♦ ♦ ♦ ♦ ♦ ♦ ♦ ♦ ♦ ♦ ♦ ♦ ♦ ♦ ♦ ♦

Start a Family Hour

Designate one afternoon a week, preferably on Saturday or Sunday, as Family Hour. Send invitations to each member of the family by Thursday and have each member RSVP. The invitation might read:

You Are Invited to Attend the [Your Surname] Family Hour

When: Sunday, November 3, 1996
Where: 23 Adams Street
Time: 3 P.M.
Refreshments will be served immediately afterward.
RSVP: By Saturday, November 2, 1996

Before each session, have the children prepare a program, such as memorizing and reciting a poem, writing and performing a skit, or thinking of a topic for a roundtable discussion, to be presented during Family Hour. Parents can get in on the act, too, by writing and reading aloud a short story, leading the family in a sing-along, or whatever their hearts desire. You can help make the Family Hour successful by making certain that sessions begin and end on time and by assigning different children to be master of ceremonies. Post a Coming Attractions bulletin on the refrigerator announcing the program for that week. This reminds children of their commitment and helps prevent the old "I forgot" excuse.

By sending and responding to the invitations, children learn social decorum. Participating in such a family ritual teaches them organization, self-esteem, how to speak before a group, planning, the importance of being on time, how to conduct a meeting, and other social skills.

◆ ◆ ◆ ◆ ◆ ◆ ◆ ◆ ◆ ◆ ◆ ◆ ◆ ◆ ◆ ◆ ◆ ◆ ◆ ◆

TRY THIS
Notes of Affirmation

Each family member takes just a moment out of his or her busy day to write each family member a short note. The notes may be placed in Dad's attaché case, Mom's suit pocket, or inside a child's notebook. Each note is a daily affirmation that each family member is special. If there has been a family disagreement, for example, a note from father to son might read: "David, I love you all the time. I disagree with your behavior today, but I know that you learned something from your mistake, and so I forgive you."

Children may write special thank-you notes to parents for the time they spend with them or for the special gifts parents or grandparents give them. Once families become accustomed to writing notes to one another, they then become more aware and mindful of negative behavior. The great thing about this procedure is that it establishes a lifetime tradition that children, in turn, pass on to their families.

◆ ◆

Share and Share Alike

At bedtime or dinnertime, have each child share with you the day's activities. Call it *Sharing Time.* Consistency is the key. If you have to travel on business and cannot be home on a regular basis, communicate with your child through E-mail, faxes, or phone calls. Remember, regardless of how busy we are, in the end it is the time we spend with our children that will really matter.

Sharing Time can include a Saturday or

Sunday evening when every family member tells of his or her contributions to the family. A child might say: "Today I made the following contributions to the family: I took out the garbage. I learned two new vocabulary words. I would like to share my papers from school with you." Mom or Dad might state: "I made the following contribution to the family: I learned not to think so much like an adult that I forget what it was like to be a child. I just want you to know that I am proud that you are my family."

You can also use this time for an art project involving the entire family. Researching and drawing a family tree, making a photo collage, or putting together a family scrapbook are all ideal projects. Display the result with pride in a prominent place in the home. Remember, no Renoir masterpiece will bring as much security and satisfaction as the family art. Remember, we are beginning with the end in mind.

Books are a great tool for Sharing Time. When you buy or borrow books for your children, look for *books that offer a wide background of knowledge.* Books on travel, people and children in other parts of the world, science, animals, how things work, art, gardening, poetry, space exploration, and air travel are best suited for Sharing Time. Develop a theme. For example, if you are reading a story about a child in Japan, have your children learn origami, or have one child research at your local library basic words in Japanese such as hello, good-bye, mother, and father. You can also have children present a pantomime or draw pictures of the stories they read. If there is a mother and father in the story, the parents should take those roles in the pantomime.

The term *family values* has been bandied about so much in the media that some might think it has become a cliché. We as parents must make sure its meaning does not become lost amid all the hype. Remember, a family is like an extension cord. Even if the cord breaks, it can be fixed through love, communication, and understanding. Talk and listen to your children and teach them to do the same with others. By doing so, the family flame will burn forever.

NOTES

Feelings

Laugh and the world laughs with you,
Weep and you weep alone,
For the sad old Earth must borrow its mirth,
But has trouble of its own.
—from the poem "Solitude"
by Ella Wheeler Wilcox

All people, at various points in their lives, feel angry, happy, sad, resentful, confident, ashamed, depressed, guilty, nervous, joyful, grouchy, worthless, or overwhelmed. It's challenging enough for adults to learn to manage their emotions; imagine what a task it must be for children. But *with enough love and effort, we can make sure our children get the practice they need to learn to deal with emotions in a healthy way.*

How I feel is what I think. We've all heard these statements from children: "I failed my test and it's all Robert's fault!" "Nobody likes me. I hate school!" And haven't you found yourself saying: "I can't do this. It's too hard"?

Feelings don't just happen by coincidence; they happen for a reason. When children are taught to understand their feelings, they will then learn how to handle them. Encourage your kids to tell you when they feel happy, mad, or sad. Take the time to listen when they say to you: "Mother, I don't like it when you yell at me. It hurts me." Or, "When you yell at me, I feel bad." When your children know that they can explain to you how they feel, you can begin to work on making your child understand the feelings. As long as you can keep children communicating, you can help them sort out their emotions.

Listen Up

Do we really listen to our children? Or do we listen in order to respond?

Children must be made to realize that they truly count. They know when they have our full attention and when they don't. Even the youngest child can discern this.

We take time to grocery shop, to do the laundry, to talk on the phone to our friends, but when do we really, really, really take the time just for our children? Set aside a time called *Listening Time*. Encourage your child to talk about what's on her or his mind during this session. Do not interrupt or interject thoughts of your own. When the child is done, resist the urge to tell her or him what to do or feel. Instead, ask: "What do you think will happen if you do that?" or "What do you think your options are?" The more you encourage your child to think critically and analytically, the more experience you are giving her or him in solving future problems.

Let your children know that whatever happens, you will be there to listen to them. How many times do we hear children say: "My parents don't understand how I feel," or "My parents never believe me"? Create the image for your children that you are not only their parent but also their best friend. Tell them that even though you sometimes disagree with their behavior, you love them unconditionally.

Remember, feelings are never right or wrong. They are simply feelings.

NOTES

Goals

Great minds have purposes,
others have wishes.
—Washington Irving

I always explain goals to children in terms of a trip to the zoo or to our favorite amusement park. Our goal, then, is not to go shopping, not to go to a friend's house, but to go to the zoo or to the amusement park. I explain that if Mom and Dad were to stop every moment to shop or to visit friends, they would never arrive at their planned destination.

It is never too early to teach children goals. Using the word *goal* on a consistent basis is extremely important. When a child does not behave in a fashion in which the parents would like them to, they may say, "Bob, you missed your goal of being all that you could today," or "Bob, you missed your goal of cleaning your room." The more the word is used, the more it will become a part of the child's permanent life tape.

Children tend to do what they see us do rather than what they hear us say. An old proverb goes: "The ant is the best teacher and it says nothing." If we want children to meet goals, they must see us as parents set and maintain goals. Allow children to hear you talk about goals for the family. For example, if you and your mate want to buy a new house, let the children hear you say, "Our goal is to buy a new house in two years. The new house will cost this or that, and in order to reach our goal, we must save this or that amount each month." The children will understand that reaching goals demands that we use restraint, discipline, and consistency in our attempts, as well as stick-to-it-iveness and determination.

◆ ◆ ◆ ◆ ◆ ◆ ◆ ◆ ◆ ◆ ◆ ◆ ◆ ◆ ◆ ◆ ◆ ◆ ◆ ◆

TRY THIS
Weekly Goals

Have each family member post her or his weekly goals on the refrigerator. A check mark is placed beside each goal that has been met for the week. Those goals that have not been met should be discussed during family meals or at a special ten-minute goal-setting family meeting, when each member can suggest ways of meeting the goals the following week.

Consistency is the key to establishing lifetime habits with children. In fact, children need guidelines and respect those teachers and parents who consistently adhere to schedules. Remember, you are recording lifetime tapes for your children. Be sure to record only those messages that you would like your children to pass on to their children.

* *

The people most able to keep their eyes on the prize are those who systematize their time, who organize the moments, the years, and the months of their lives. We must ask our children: What is your goal in life? Is it to watch television? To play video games? To sleep? To play? Questions like these get children thinking about the time they waste and how that time can best be used. Furthermore, we parents must practice what we preach. How many of us have wasted this precious raw material? The anonymous poem below says it all in just a few lines. Think about it.

Time

One minute; sixty seconds in it
Didn't choose it; had it forced upon me
I can either use it or abuse it
For my life and eternity is in it.

NOTES

_____

_____

_____

_____

_____

_____

Habit

How use does breed the habit in
a man or woman.
> —Shakespeare,
> *Two Gentlemen of Verona*

Just as a journey of a thousand miles begins with a single step, so the journey of life must begin with children learning to take Olympian steps in the journey they have chosen in life. Children need to learn early that if we are to get "there," we must begin "here."

That which we do daily and consistently becomes a lifetime habit. How many times have we heard parents say: "Where did I go wrong?" Once children or adults become lost because they had the wrong maps of life, it is a difficult process to get back on track.

As the old adage goes, we must reap what we sow. We sow a thought and reap an action. We sow the action and reap a habit. We sow the habit and reap our destiny.

. . . .

TRY THIS

Planting the Seeds of Habit

In a flowerpot or your backyard garden, have your children plant seeds or bulbs. Tell them to water and nourish the plants and watch them grow. Say to them: "You see, we sowed a seed and we reaped a plant." This is the way it is in life: What we sow is what we reap.

. . . .

Habits should be tied into the goals of your family mission statement (see Direction). Remember, this means that you, the parent, must eradicate bad habits. You must also seek the Olympic gold. This does not mean that the journey will be an easy one. When we see a winner standing proudly in the winning circle, few of us stop to think about the excruciating journey that led him or her to this triumphant place. Let us remind our children what these winners have endured and overcome in the past to make the present possible. The satisfaction of conquering these challenges makes all the hard work and pain worthwhile. On the day of victory, none of us is tired.

We all have the potential to become winners, but only when we lose the losing attitude. *The attitude determines the altitude.* What altitude do you want for your child? What altitude do you want for your family? It all begins with a single positive step. That step must be taken now, this moment, today. That step must be reinforced tomorrow, and tomorrow, and yes, tomorrow until you can truly say: "We made it, we did it."

Nipping Boredom in the Bud

On those inevitable days when children chant over and over, "Where are we going today?" "There's nothing to do," and "I'm bored," encourage them to think of ways to entertain themselves, to create their own mind puzzles. Establish an I Am Bored Center in your home as an alternative to playing video games or watching television.

The I Am Bored Center can involve the following activities:

- **Poetry Fun.** Make copies of poems studied during Sharing Time (see Family). Have the kids write down what certain lines from the poem mean to them. They can also draw pictures illustrating what they think the poem means.

- **The Results of My Thinking.** This is an activity where children must think on a certain subject for twenty minutes, then write down their ideas and conclusions.

- **Consider All Possibilities (CAP).** Here, children read a story and then try to think of alternative endings. This procedure is called "Doing a CAP." Encourage your children to apply the practice in their daily lives.

- **If I Could.** Have the children write down their thoughts on things they would do if they could. This may be done in the form of a wish list. They should also be encouraged to write what they are willing to do to make their wishes come true. This becomes a lesson in realizing that it takes hard work to make dreams come true.

Keep the paperwork from all the activities in different-colored folders. Logic and brainteaser books are also good to have on hand, as well as jigsaw puzzles, word games, and other materials that foster creative thinking.

It may take some time to build up the I Am Bored Center, but you will find that your child will make a habit of going to this center when he or she announces, "I am bored." Not only will your children become more academically adept, but they will also learn that none of us has to remain bored.

DON'T FORGET TO EVALUATE AND PRAISE YOUR CHILDREN'S WORK

Just as adults respond positively to praise, children likewise enjoy hearing that they are bright, wonderful, and great. If children know that the work they complete will be noticed or rewarded with positive affirmation, they will feel the incentive to finish it. The consistency with which you check your child's work will determine their consistency in using the I Am Bored Center. Purchase colorful, decorative stickers that you can place on your children's work. Writing brief notes to your child ("I am so proud of you. You are so bright. I love you.") and leaving them in the I Am Bored Center are also strong motivators.

NOTES

If It's to Be, It's Up to Me

No one will care as much about me as
I must care about myself.
—from the Westside
Preparatory School creed

Whenever you point a finger, remember that three fingers are pointing right back at you. Teach every child that progress begins with "I and me," not "you, them, and they." Don't be so quick to blame others. Encourage your child to begin conversations with: "I made the wrong choice. This is what happened, and here is what I conclude."

Suppose your child has a fight with a friend and proclaims, "Maggie does not like me. She hates me!" By reassuring your child that she is a good person and that her family and other friends love her, you are teaching her to think and say in the future, "Maggie will never know what she is missing by not having me as a friend, and I feel sorry for anyone who does not have a wonderful person like me for a friend." An alternative to help put things in different perspective is to ask your child, "What is the worst thing that can happen to you if Maggie never talks to you again?" Or, "Will you be better off or worse off without her friendship?" Here you are teaching your child to consider all factors, not just the factor of Maggie not being her friend. You are relieving the child of having to feel responsible for someone else's behavior or someone else's response.

We often become defensive about claiming ownership to something we have done because we fear unpleasant reprisal. When children learn that it is okay to say "I did this and I am sorry, and I learned from what I did. I will not do that again because..." they will learn to take responsibility for their actions. The finger pointing and blame usually come from children and adults alike who have a poor sense of self and who feel that if they admit blame it will lessen their sense of self. The more secure the self, the more secure one is to admit defeats and wrongs.

Just as we would not expect our physician to prescribe medication before he or she diagnoses our malady, we, as parents, should refrain from trying to find an instant remedy. Why do our children repeatedly lie, steal, or behave in an overt manner? Have we given our children secure outlets for their feelings? *Secure children do not point fingers or lie or steal.* Insecure children pretend to be afraid of nothing yet are afraid of everything.

The fewer negative messages your child receives, the less likely he or she is to become a defensive finger pointer. Think for a moment of the times some callous person has said to you: "My, you have large feet," "You eat like a pig," "Can't you do anything right?" "What did you do *this* time?" "Not *you* again." The more we hear such things, the more we are inclined to believe them. *Negativity therefore becomes a self-perpetuating hierarchy.* Words can kill as surely as weapons.

The word *responsible* does mean "able to respond." What lessons have we taught our children that give them too few ways with which to respond to everyday situations? How often have we taught our children to say, "It's not my fault"? We live in a society in which the average talk-show host interviews "victim" after "victim." *Have we led our children to believe that we are now a faultless society?*

When children do poorly in school, it is easy to blame someone else instead of simply asking, "Did you really do your best? If someone else is to blame, would you like to get even with that person? We can get even, you know, by succeeding." Or, "How would you like to prove your teacher wrong by getting all the answers right on your next test? Can you imagine how your teacher will feel when she thinks you will make a poor grade on your next test, and you get all perfect grades? What do you think you will need to do to make this happen? Are you willing to really, really shock your teacher by succeeding?" This method does not allow your child to give in to being a "victim"; it forces children to seek alternatives.

"If it's to be, it's up to me" is the winning attitude. Deformity is the first step toward suppression. To truly deform children is to allow them to become "victims."

• •

TRY THIS
Attitude Adjustment

Talk to your child about what it means to live in vain. To live in vain is to do nothing to make the world a better place. To live in vain is to always look for what others can do for you, rather than asking what you can do for others. *To live in vain is to take the attitude that it is always someone else's fault rather than looking within yourself.*

• •

NOTES

_____

_____

_____

_____

_____

Image

> *If there is anything that we wish to change in the child, we should first examine it and see whether it is not something that could be better changed in ourselves.*
> —Carl Gustav Jung

What is your image as a parent? As a teacher? Do your children already know what you are going to say before you say it? This is called an image. It determines how people will respond to you. *What is the image as a parent that you hold in your children's eyes? Take the time to repeatedly and consistently reinforce the image you would like to have.*

I once asked my students why they behaved for me. I said: "I do not beat you, I do not yell, I do not punish." They replied: "We behave because we know you will not take our misbehaving." How did I relate this message? When I first started to teach thirty years ago in the infamous Delano School on Chicago's fetid Westside, I let the students know right away that I was dead serious that I would leave no child behind. The children knew that I expected standard English and standard behavior. They knew I was like a fine Swiss watchmaker: I knew every minute what I was going to teach. I gave my message loud and clear: "You have the right to fail, but not in my classroom. You have the right to be a mediocre student, but the student has not been born who will make me a mediocre teacher."

Keep in mind, though, that mixed messages don't work. It is very important that parents work together to give children the same script. If Mother reprimands by saying, "Tracy, life is all about the choices we make. If you choose not to clean your room, I then have the right to choose not to take you to the zoo on Saturday," and Father later says, "Tracy, I am tired of telling you the same thing over and over again. You will not go to the zoo on Saturday," Tracy will understandably be confused as to exactly why she isn't going to the zoo. Just as we have business meetings to discuss strategy, we must also devise and implement family strategies that will best enhance our images as parents.

I remember one young student of mine during my second year of teaching. At the age of eight, he had already been labeled a thief. The other children warned me on the first day of school to beware of Kirk because he was a thief. I defiantly said: "I just do not believe that Kirk is a thief. Kirk," I said, "I want you to be in charge of my purse for the entire year." Needless to say, not one thing was stolen the entire year, not only from my purse but also from any child. Suppose I as a teacher had led the class in perpetuating the image that Kirk was a thief. By removing the negative image, Kirk blossomed into one of the brightest achievers in my class.

Remember, do not become a good parent and a good teacher only for your children. Become a good parent for yourself. Pursue excellence for excellence' sake. Be all that you can be as a parent. What better role model can you provide than being a confident, secure individual who recognizes that everyone should be valued—children and adults alike?

◆ ◆

TRY THIS
The Boy Who Cried Wolf

To reinforce the concept of image, read the story of the Boy Who Cried Wolf to your child. Start a discussion by asking, "What image did this little boy have? What happens when we tell lies? What did you learn from reading this story?"

◆ ◆

NOTES

_____

_____

_____

_____

_____

_____

_____

Individuality

In a world where everybody is like everybody else, the hardest thing in the world is to be me.

—e. e. cummings

From the time children begin school, they are taught to be members of the pack. They hold hands, they line up, they are told to get along with the others, they are taught to share. *In all of this "sharing and getting along," children often lose their sense of self.* When there is no self, we then become other people's selves. We teach our children to be a part of the pack and then we chastise them later for wanting to do whatever the pack does. Is there any wonder, then, that our children rebel?

When do we teach children what and when to share? Do we share our paychecks with people who sat idly while we worked? Do we share our food in collective stomachs? Do we share our homes with the homeless? Do we share our cars with people without cars? Do we share our families? This, to me, is why children become so confused with our teachings. We teach them one thing and they see us do another. We force them to share toys, and they see us not sharing with the homeless person on the street corner. We force them to get along with one another, and they hear of our adult battles and anarchy and crime on television and in our daily conversations. They begin to think that we are merely word spillers and not doers. Is there any question that the average child then seeks the approval of the pack? Isn't it the same pack we introduced them to?

If we hear the word *maladjusted* in connection with our child, we think there is something wrong with him or her. Think for a moment. Often it is the "maladjusted" among us who make a difference for everyone else. The person who steps away from the crowd, who looks for his or her own way, is the one who forges a new path for others to follow. The lofty eagle never travels in a flock but soars majestically to great heights on its own.

Every pure and lofty spirit was labeled

maladjusted. Copernicus was maladjusted. Henry Ford was maladjusted. Louis Pasteur was maladjusted. Anesthesia was considered sinful, and today we couldn't possibly contemplate surgery without it. People who are maladjusted are those who make the biggest difference in other people's lives. I was maladjusted as a teacher in the Chicago public school system. I refused to believe that every child could not learn to read, write, and compute. That belief system has never failed me. More often than not, it has been my maladjusted students who have grown up to become scholars and significant contributors to society. In fact, one of my most maladjusted students, Erika McCoy, was shown on the TV news program "60 Minutes" graduating from Norfolk State University summa cum laude. How's *that* for maladjustment?

The child who has a good sense of self does not need to plug in to others for survival. From the time we are conceived, our mothers eat for us. They sleep for us. They nurture and care for our every need. Then comes birth. Wow, we are born into this new world where we know nobody. We are unplugged and unsure of what to do. We therefore constantly go through life trying to find a place in which to make a connection. The only time we cease seeking an outlet is when we find that we have within our own selves what we are seeking from others. The sooner children discover this, the sooner they set the rules for the pack rather than following the rules. In other words, they become "maladjusted" enough to dare to trust the most miraculous person on earth: themselves. The sooner they can declare, "I am me and that is all I need to be," the sooner they can truly be free.

We as parents often think that discovering our self has something to do with our socio-economic level, the kind of home we live in, the neighborhood in which we live, or the expensive schools our children attend. Ironically, however, it is these things that can actually make children feel worse about themselves. A child can say: "I have toys, money, clothing, a nice house, and a nice car, but I am still miserable." Children who feel this way have never discovered the miracle of self.

◆ ◆

TRY THIS
Take Your Child to the Land of Oz

Read with your child the classic book *The Wizard of Oz.* Like many children, the characters in this beloved story come to learn that they are seeking what they already have. Nothing in the world can replace self-esteem.

◆ ◆

NOTES

_____

_____

_____

_____

_____

_____

Jealousy

To be jealous of another person is to admit that I do not like me.
—Marva Collins

*E*ach of us is born unique. I believe there is no one on this earth who is quite like me—no one with my nose, my hair, my height, my eyes, my family background, and all the strengths and weaknesses that make me me. As long as I feel this is true, I will not want to be like anyone else. I will not envy others. I respect each person for her or his uniqueness, but I never, never want to give up my uniqueness to be them. This is what we teach our children at Westside Prep. When a student calls another student a name, the latter is taught to respond, "I am sorry you feel that way, but I will not empower your negativity." The first child must then take his or her plug elsewhere, for the outlet he or she attempted to plug in to did not work. When enough outlets are refused the perpetrator, she or he then gives up trying to find them and learns to concentrate on the wonderful person within.

We also teach our students to become both the program and the tape each of us carries in every endeavor. We believe, as Ralph Waldo Emerson said, "Envy is ignorance, imitation is suicide, and we have each been given our plot of ground on which to till. That no nourishing kernel of corn will come to us except that plot which we have done the tilling." Emerson's famous essay "Self-Reliance" is required reading for our students beginning in the third grade. From this great classic, they learn to believe in their own thoughts, to believe that what is true for them in their own hearts is true for all people.

That which we leave unattended goes unattended. We teach our children all the happily-ever-after stories, but most American academic programs do not deal with the real world. We must teach our children stories of what happens when jealousy takes over. The greatest story in the world on jealousy is the biblical story of Joseph. Despite the envy of his brothers, Joseph concentrated on being all that he could be. He overcame evil by succeeding.

The same brothers who were jealous of him, who had sold him into slavery, were eventually forced to come to him for help.

Young children begin very early to form cliques that exclude those they do not like, but many times the child who is ostracized from the clique or the peer group is the child who, for one reason or another, has unwittingly inspired jealousy in his or her classmates, perhaps simply for being different. Jealousy usually springs from our own inadequacies. Any time we feel that someone else has what we would like to have, the green-eyed monster of envy appears.

When I was a child growing up in rural Alabama, some of the girls at school often threatened to beat me up. I couldn't go to the washroom without being threatened or picked on. At the time this was happening, I thought something was wrong with me. I felt alienated and I retreated by becoming an avid reader. Jealousy, in this case, propelled me to succeed. Years later I met one of these former classmates during one of my lecture tours, and she revealed, "We were always jealous of you because you did not speak the way the rest of us did, and because you got praise from all the teachers, and you got the biggest part in all the school plays, and you never got in trouble at school. You always made the rest of us look bad."

Many times the superachievers in our school become the targets of jealousy. When that happens, I ask the children: "If you were stranded on an island, and one child in this room could save you, which child would you choose to save you?" The answer, of course, is always the child who is the superachiever.

I then say, "Now, I know there are some of you who are jealous of Ann or Tom, and I must ask you, what do you think you need to do in order to have some of those qualities you envy in that person?" I also ask, "Does jealousy get you where you would like to be? If not, what must you do to get there?" With this drill, the children learn that the time it takes to be jealous could be used to reach our goals and our life destination. Students write compositions or make lists of the children they are jealous of and why, and then they write down what they intend to do to get where they would like to be in life.

Jealousy keeps each of us from reaching the destination we were put on earth to reach. While we are envying what someone else has or is, we are missing the bus that will take us farther on our own journey. Each of us is the unique piece of the total puzzle that is the human race.

With my own three children, Cynthia, Patrick, and Eric, I reminded them each day of their wonderful and unique selves. I also gave one day a week to each child. That child could decide what he or she wanted to do on that special day. I never compared one child to another, but I did explain to them that it takes special pieces to complete a picture, and each of them was a piece of that total picture.

Dealing with Jealous Siblings

How we communicate with children during their formative years often depends on the relationships they have with others. Say one of your children receives a good report card, while another did not do as well. Tell the first child, "I am so proud of you. You are so bright." Say to the other child, "I like the grade you got in this subject, but don't you think we could do better in that subject?" Notice the "we." When an admirer says to one child, "You are such a good-looking child," and ignores child number two, the parent should say, "Yes, I agree Mark is very handsome, but isn't Ryan handsome also?" This way you are reminding the unthinking admirer that both children count. You are alleviating future jealousy between siblings.

If a new child is born into the household, it is not enough to say, "Why are you jealous of your little sister or brother?" We should say: "You know, Robert, I am really going to need your help in caring for the new baby. How do you think you can help me? Remember, without your help, I will not know what to do." You are not only asking for help, but you are also expanding your child's ability to think. He now must drop the "I am jealous" feeling and put on a new thinking cap. The emotional pain of jealousy begins to disappear, and a new feeling of "I am needed" has been put in its place.

◆ ◆ ◆ ◆ ◆ ◆ ◆ ◆ ◆ ◆ ◆ ◆ ◆ ◆ ◆ ◆ ◆ ◆ ◆ ◆

TRY THIS
The Lemon Squeeze

This is a Collins family tradition. *Feelings can only be changed when they are dealt with.* Hold a thirty-minute family meeting called a Lemon Squeeze, in which each family member is allowed to say, "You know, Joe, I am jealous of you because…" The other can respond, "Well, I am jealous of you because…" Each child in this way discovers that spoken jealousies can show us our uniqueness, and that jealousies are sometimes unfounded. No revelations, however, are to be labeled stupid or ridiculous. If we feel it, it is real to us. Ask, "What can I do that you will not feel this jealousy?"

♦ ♦

TRY THIS
To Be or Not to Be… Jealous

Borrowing a line from Shakespeare's *Hamlet*, we can further address the jealousy issue. Give your children blank sheets of paper. In one column, have them list all the reasons they are jealous of someone. In the next column, they can write all the reasons they should not be jealous of that someone.

♦ ♦

NOTES

Kindness and Compassion

Be kind to everyone you meet. It just may be God's angel in disguise.
—Marva Collins

When we suggest to our children that they should be kind, do they really grasp this abstract concept? *Kindness is not an act but a daily habit. The more we practice being kind, the better we will feel about ourselves.*

Young people should be reminded that not every act of kindness receives gratitude, but that is not the reason we practice kindness. A child who is kind may earn the label Goody Two Shoes. Tell your kids that the friends who tease them for being kind have not yet discovered the good feeling that comes from inside when we are kind to others. Being kind is pretty much like touching a hot stove. Often children do not believe the stove is hot until they personally touch it for themselves. From that moment on, they become dedicated to telling others that stoves are indeed hot, and yes, they do burn. Likewise, only when we discover the magic of kindness and how good we feel inside do we become addicted to finding something kind to do each day.

Suggest that your children do one kind act a day. They may want to keep a file of the kind deeds done each day, or record them in a journal. These acts might be as simple as taking out the garbage one day a week for another sibling without telling the other sibling they have done it. It might be helping a neighbor carry groceries, shoveling snow for a friend, or cleaning a sister's or brother's room.

Many times children will remind their brother or sister of the things they have done for him or her and request a favor in return. Children should be taught that we do not do kind things because we expect others to return our kindness. We are kind because the most important person is us, the most important time is now, and the most important thing on earth is to do good. We practice kindness to make ourselves feel good. When the self inside feels good, we automatically make others feel good.

◆ ◆

TRY THIS
Kindness Through Literature

If you have not read the story of "Beauty and the Beast" to your children, consider doing so. In this beautiful tale, kindness makes a phenomenal difference and shows that we can never judge a book by its cover. In the story, children will see that not only was Beauty beautiful, but she also had a good heart, and that beneath the Beast's frightful appearance was a handsome prince. "The Frog Prince," about a girl kind enough to kiss the frog that eventually becomes a prince, is another story of kindness.

There is a wealth of books, stories, and poems that teach kindness. I suggest the poem "Kind Words." The fable "Androcles and the Lion" illustrates that little people can often befriend adults or older people. Oscar Wilde's *The Happy Prince* is another popular story of kindness. The book *Love You Forever* by Robert Munsch is a good tool for teaching compassion. By reading "The Little Match Girl" by Hans Christian Andersen, children will learn to feel the pain of another and that kindness is perhaps one of our greatest attributes. This is a wonderful story to share at Christmastime when far too many of us have taught children that Christmas is about what we receive, not what we give.

♦ ♦

To create the framework for becoming a kind adult, children need daily lessons in compassion and caring for others. Children learn from examples. You may want to ask your child or children the following: "Someone yells at you and calls you a name. How do you feel? Do you feel sad or happy? Meanwhile, someone else says, 'What a lovely dress. You are such a pretty girl.' Which statement makes you feel sad? Which statement makes you feel happy?"

The anonymous poem below was given to me by my grandmother when I was four years of age. You may want to post it in your child's room.

If You Were

If you were busy being kind,
Before you knew it, you would find
You'd soon forget to think 'twas true
That someone was unkind to you.

If you were busy being glad
And cheering people who are sad,
Although your heart may ache a bit,
You'd soon forget to notice it.

If you were busy being good
And doing the best you could,
You'd not have time to blame some man
Who's doing just the best he can.

If you were busy being right,
You'd find yourself too busy quite
To criticize your neighbor long
Because he's busy being wrong.

Once children practice kindness and reap its rewards, the lesson will last forever. The exquisite words of Emily Dickinson perhaps say it best:

If I can stop one Heart from breaking
I shall not live in Vain
If I can ease one Life the Aching
Or cool one Pain
Or help one fainting robin
Unto his Nest again
I shall not live in Vain.

NOTES

_____

_____

_____

_____

*L*earning

A little learning is a dangerous thing.
Drink deep, or taste not.
— Alexander Pope

Your home is your child's first school, and you are your child's first teacher. The word *teacher* is from the Latin word meaning "to lead," or to draw out. *You must learn to lead your youngster toward learning in every endeavor.*

Help to develop your child's language by verbalizing often. For example, when your child puts on his or her socks, say, "You are putting your red sock on your left foot; you are putting your red sock on your right foot." Point out objects in your surroundings: "This is detergent; it cleans our clothing. This is bleach; it takes the stains from our clothing."

Foster inquisitiveness in children by asking, "What do you think makes the television work? The radio? The stove? The refrigerator?"

When children learn to ask when, why, which one, and how many, they are developing their very first comprehension skills. *Comprehension comes easier for children when they learn very early to have an inquiring mind.*

◆ ◆

TRY THIS
Travel Games

When you are out driving with your children, set a goal for them. For example, Michael will count all black cars, and Anne will count all Mercedes or Buicks. Small gifts may be given to the winner. To make certain that every child is a winner (remember, just participating in the game and being able to focus mean something), small gifts should go to the second winner, third winner, and so on.

To teach directions while driving, point out: "This is Adams Street, and we are turning onto Elm Street. We are going south." After doing this several times, invite the children to tell you which direction you are traveling.

◆ ◆

It is not a cliché to begin dinnertime discussions with "What did you learn today?" If this becomes a continual exercise, children will become open to learning. Praise your children's responses by saying, "My, you are such great learners. I am so proud of all of you. Now let me tell you what I learned today."

If another driver cuts you off in traffic, the temptation is usually to do the same to that driver or to another driver. Instead, ask your child, "What did we learn from this?" Encourage your child to reason that two wrongs do not make a right. Ask what might have happened had you given in to your desire to "get back" at the driver.

* *

TRY THIS
Shopping Lessons

The grocery store is an excellent learning place. Ask children: "Which container do you think holds the most?" Show them a short, squatty container as opposed to a tall container, and guide them to realize that the size of the container is not necessarily directly related to its volume.

Ask questions such as "I have twenty dollars to spend on vegetables. If I buy one pound of cabbage at $1.25 per pound, one bag of carrots at $2.25 per bag, and six ears of corn for $1.05, how much change will I have left from the twenty dollars?"

Have your children help prepare weekly written menus. Give each child an opportunity to prepare menus for the week. Each child must prepare the menu a week in advance. Confer with the child as to what nutritional value is contained in each menu. This is a wonderful way to teach spelling, writing, and planning. Accompany the children to the supermarket to buy the groceries, and let them handle the money at the checkout counter.

◆ ◆

Putting Math in a Positive Light

Math tends to scare most children and even adults. The way we see the problem is the problem. The image given children about numbers and math is how they will view the problem throughout their lives. It's never too early to put a positive spin on math. You can start by teaching your child that fractions are simply things that are not whole. For example, tell them, "When you give your sister or brother half of your pizza, half of your toys, or half of your treats, you are now dealing in fractions. If you have a whole dollar, and you spend fifty cents of that dollar, you no longer have a whole dollar. One half of the dollar is now gone. One half plus one half equals one whole."

Mom buys a box of cookies. There are twelve cookies in the package. Three friends come to visit. They all would like to share your cookies with you. This means that the cookies are no longer a whole twelve cookies. They have been divided up among four of you. How many cookies will each of you get? Each of you will get three cookies. Four threes equal a total of twelve.

Fractions are like dividing the cookies. The more parts you divide the whole into, the more pieces of fractions, or parts, you will have. A boy has a set of eight trains. Four of the trains work, and four of the trains do not work. What fraction of the trains work? One half of the set of trains work, and one half of the set do not work. How many trains does the boy have in all? He has eight trains, and one half of eight is four.

Have the children cut one whole sheet of paper into halves, then fourths, then eighths, then sixteenths. Show them that the more pieces into which the paper is divided, the smaller the pieces, and the fewer pieces cut, the larger the portions. Before you begin the activity, ask your child: "Which would you rather have, one tenth or one half?" He or she will probably say, "One tenth," until the child starts cutting and sees that one tenth is much smaller than one half. Children hear the word "tenth" and assume that it is larger than "half." Measuring cups are an ideal tool for learning fractions. You can also use building blocks. Say to your child: "Give me one fourth of your twelve blocks," and so on.

Move forward with questions such as: "What fraction of the windows are facing north? What fraction of the windows are facing east?" Remember, no term is too difficult for even the youngest child's understanding if we use the same terminology over and over again. Repetition and drill are the key to educating even the slowest or youngest child.

When the monthly bills come, help your children understand that bills are part of life. By the time children are five years of age, they should become involved in the bill-paying process. Begin by having them learn to sort. They can sort all the utility bills together, all the food bills together, all the clothing bills together, and all the mortgage bills together. Have them add up each set of bills. This gives children a more informed perspective when they hear you say, "We can't afford it." When you think they are old enough, give your children the responsibility of writing one or two checks per month (naturally, they should fill in everything but the signature). This also teaches writing and number skills, order, sequence, and cause and effect. Children learn that the funds in the account diminish as checks are written.

Fractions will not frighten your child if they have become comfortable with the concept at home, and it only takes a few minutes of *consistent, persistent* time to do this.

Make learning a priority in your home and in the classroom. If children know that learning is important to you, they will continuously try to please you. I remember my students coming into my classroom in the morning and saying, "Mrs. Collins, let me tell you what I learned last night." Let us encourage our children to think, to imagine, and, most of all, to value learning as a lifetime pursuit.

NOTES

_____

_____

_____

_____

_____

_____

_____

_____

_____

Manners

Thank you, please, excuse me, *and
I am sorry say more about us than
all our outward apparel.*
　　　　　　　　—Marva Collins

Nowadays, *please, thank you,* and *forgive me* are words that seem to have gone the way of the last dinosaur. When was the last time you heard someone say: "That child has such good manners"? Manners are a form of discipline. Without them, we'd be like wild horses.

In a world that celebrates the attitude of "If it feels good, do it," our children must be awfully confused as to what is right and what is wrong, what is proper and what is improper. *There are numerous ways to teach your child proper manners that they will take with them on their journey to adulthood.*

When your child does what you ask or does a favor for you, say, "Thank you. I don't know what I would do without your help."

Practice saying "Excuse me" and "Please" to your child. Remember, never forget that you are making a lifetime tape. Whatever you put on that tape is what your child will go through life playing.

When you answer the phone, teach politeness by saying: "Hello, this is the Jones residence. May I help you, please?" If the person being called is not at home, tell your child to always have paper and pencil handy to take a message. Encourage your child to repeat the number to the caller to avoid mistakes. Teach your child to end the conversation by saying, "I am sorry you missed my parents. I am sure they will want to return your call. Have a great day." These kinds of manners put your child above being "average." Remember, average people are never in short supply; we can find them anywhere.

Take the time to teach your children to knock before entering a sibling's room, and to ask permission to use belongings that are not theirs. In other words, they must respect others as they would like to be respected.

We all like to receive. Children should be taught, however, that not only must we give in order to receive, but we must also acknowledge what we have received. Instill in your children that thank-you notes should be sent for birthday gifts, holiday gifts, or any gift received.

* *

TRY THIS
When Bad Manners Persist

When children persist in showing bad manners, they should have a place in the home in which to retreat and write a hundred reasons why they are too bright to exhibit such behavior. This causes children to look into the positive gifts that are inside themselves rather than belaboring the negative act.

* *

Today's children know very little about respecting their elders. Teach your child to stand when grown-ups enter the room and to be seated when told: "You may be seated." Teach your child to ask to be excused from the dinner table or from family meals.

Sharing is part of being a civilized,

well-mannered individual. Therefore, teach your children to be good hosts. Encourage them to share with their friends but to protect their rights when it appears other children may destroy their toys. Teach them to say, "I am glad you are my friend, and I am glad you have come to play with me, but you must take care of my toys, or I will have to put them away."

Below is a Good Manners checklist for you and your child to keep.

AT HOME

♦ Know and practice table manners: Do not begin to eat until the entire family is seated. Close your mouth when chewing. Break bread before eating. Use a napkin. Do not stretch at the table. Ask to be excused if you must leave the table before everyone else has finished. Say, "Mom or Dad, I like the meal you prepared. Thank you for a wonderful meal."

♦ When coughing or sneezing, cover your mouth and say "Excuse me."

♦ When friends visit, do not eat without offering them whatever you are eating.

- Put your clothing away after undressing.

- Put the cap back on the toothpaste after using.

- Wash out the bathtub after using.

AT SCHOOL

- Know when to refuse or accept treats or anything else.

- Preface a request with "May I please?"

- Know when to use "No, thank you" and "Yes, thank you."

- Say "Pardon" when passing in front of a person.

- Return to owner an article he or she dropped.

- Practice attentive manners when your classmates are speaking.

- Be willing to accept criticism.

- Show consideration for others (handicapped, elderly, teachers).

- Know how to give and answer a courteous greeting.

- Play fair; do not be a cheat.

- Do not interrupt a conversation.

- Do not write on desks, buildings, or walls.

- Keep your desk tidy; it represents you; it is your home away from home.

- Follow instructions from the teacher.

- Help anyone smaller than yourself who might need help.

- Never bully anyone.

- Treat others the way you would like to be treated. Remember, if something hurts you or bothers you, it bothers others, too.

- Never let others take away your self; it is yours for life.

AT A PARTY OR SOMEONE ELSE'S HOME

- Greet the host or hostess and thank him or her for inviting you.

- Do not run into parts of the home where you are not invited.

- Know when to say, "No, thank you, I have had plenty."

- If you desire second portions, say, "Mrs. Jones, may I please have another piece of cake?"

- Enter into the fun with good spirit. Do not attempt to take all the host or hostess's time for yourself. Learn to share.

- Do not make negative comments about the food. If you do not like something, simply say, "No, thank you, I have eaten already," but never "I don't like that."

- When leaving, say to the host or hostess: "I had a wonderful time. The food was wonderful. Thank you so much for inviting me."

- Conduct yourself properly so that people will want to invite you again. This means practicing good behavior so that people will be sad rather than happy to see you leave.

- Send a thank-you note to the host or hostess.

IN PUBLIC

- Do not talk loudly during movies, plays, or other public events.

- Walk to the right in hallways.

- When shopping, touch only merchandise you plan to buy.

- Do not throw garbage anywhere but in a trash can.

- If someone pushes the button in the elevator for you, say "Thank you."

- If you accidentally bump into someone, say gently: "Please excuse me, I am so sorry."

- Never point or jeer at others.

- When walking on the sidewalk, make room for others to pass.

- Help elderly people cross the street. Offer to carry packages for the elderly.

- Offer to help the handicapped.

- If someone offers money for your act of kindness, say, "No, thank you, the pleasure was all mine."

- Never, never, never walk and eat on the street at the same time.

- Cross at the corner or in crosswalks.

SUPER MANNERS

- Always respect the rights of others.

- Have patience with other people's points of view.

- Keep house and room in order.

- Respect the hard work of your parents.

- Wipe your shoes on the doormat before entering your home or the homes of others.

- Learn to carry on a meaningful, entertaining, nonnegative conversation. Never speak ill of anyone not present during the conversation.

- Never gossip.

- Make new children to your neighborhood or school feel welcome.

- Use "thank you," "please," and "excuse me" when appropriate.

By working closely with your young one on this checklist and giving praise and encouragement—not to mention being diligent in practicing these same manners yourself—you will create the image of a well-bred, intelligent, above-average child.

NOTES

_____

_____

_____

_____

_____

_____

_____

_____

_____

Negativity

Once a word is said, it can never be taken away. Think before we speak, love before we hate.
                                    —Marva Collins

Never forget that you, the parent, are being recorded. You are recording your values daily on the mind of your child. Whatever you tape will become a lifetime tape.

Think how many times a child will draw a picture and the parent will say: "What is it?" The very words "What is it?" already say to your child, "Your picture is not very good because I did not know what it was." Say instead, "What a wonderful picture! Tell me about it."

How often we begin to reprimand with the word *Don't*. "Don't do this; don't do that." Try instead, "I think you are making the wrong choice, bright one. Can you think of a better choice?"

Use every opportunity you can to teach your child to think positively. If your child chances to say, "Alan makes me sick," encourage him or her to say instead: "I like Alan, but I do not like it when he does this or that." Positive affirmation of others makes us feel better. Tell your child: "When we speak negatively of others, we too feel bad. Think for a moment what would happen if Mom or Dad gave twenty people a battery jump from our car battery. Soon, our own car, too, would not start." The same is true in our relationships. When we give negatives to others, we drain our own batteries, and soon we too will not "start." Therefore, we must never allow someone else to drain our energies so that we feel bad.

Not only are you helping your child develop a powerful vocabulary with the words above, but you are recording an "I am wonderful" tape for her or him. If your child believes he or she is inspiring, foremost, momentous, brilliant, and wonderful, he or she will begin to develop a behavior that fits the image you have provided. Negative and hurtful words will help children create a negative image. Just as we are what we eat, we are also what we hear and do.

A poem by Emily Dickinson sums up these beliefs:

He ate and drank the precious Words—
His Spirit grew robust—
He knew no more that he was poor,
Nor that his frame was Dust—

He danced along the dingy Days
and this Bequest of Wings
Was but a Book—What Liberty
A loosened spirit brings—

Remember, words can destroy your child, or they can become a powerful tape for success. We are what we are because of the choices we make. Help your child learn to make positive, happy choices.

* * * * * * * * * * * * * * * * * *

TRY THIS
Word Power

Tell your child that she or he is awesome, brilliant, smart, bright, and phenomenal. Bring out the positive by expressing: "You are a gem. You are astounding. You are inspiring. You are empowering. You are excellence. Your excellence is contagious. You are a mentally gifted minor. You are pleasant. You are a joy. You are a creator. You are fantastic. You are momentous. You are spectacular." The list goes on and on.

* * * * * * * * * * * * * * * * * *

NOTES

_____

_____

_____

_____

_____

Organization

*That which is organized does not have
to be found.*
—Marva Collins

Pose the following questions to your children: "Can you imagine how you would feel if God had put your head where your feet are? If your ears were where your nose is?" Explain that this is called organization. Everything has its place.

Many toys come with small pieces that sometimes end up in the vacuum cleaner or the trash can. How many Barbie shoes have become a part of the household trash? Teach your children that with every right comes a responsibility. Toys should be kept in order in their rightful containers. This is the first lesson children learn in a lifetime of organizing. As a teacher, I have known many families who were constantly late for school and work because the child could not find their other shoe, or the parent could not find the car keys or some other needed object.

You can explain organization to your children this way: "Can you imagine if I prepared dinner by putting the macaroni and cheese in with the broccoli and the soup, and then mixed in Jell-O? We would have a mess, wouldn't we? Well, this is what happens when we are unorganized. We organize our preparation of food, and likewise, we must organize our lives, or they, too, become one big blob of a mess."

• •

TRY THIS
Made to Order

Use folders of different colors to hold your child's schoolwork. Teach your child to place "done" work in these folders and keep them in a specific place in your home for review and Sharing Time (see Family). Have a specific place for children to put their toys, books, and other personal belongings before they begin the nighttime ritual of going to bed.

Help children organize their book bags. As a

teacher, I have seen book bags filled with crumpled papers and papers never reviewed by parents. Some children have even carried around an entire year's work without ever emptying their book bags. I often think how much this is like real life. Some people carry around years and years of unresolved problems without emptying their brain of this baggage.

* *

In an empty shoe box, place a variety of pennies, nickels, dimes, and quarters, along with paper clips, old buttons, rubber bands, ballpoint pens, and other miscellaneous items. Mix up the items. Tell your child he or she can keep all the quarters he or she can find in the box in five minutes. This activity demonstrates that we are always struggling to find what would be much easier had we organized all the quarters together, all the nickels, and so forth. Say that this is what happens when we do not put our socks, shoes, and other items into their proper places.

Ask, "What happens when things are not in order?" Teach your child to respond and repeat, "When things are not in order, we have disorder, and disorder means to be unorganized." Give your child encouragement by saying, "Good job! You are so bright."

Humor helps in getting a point across: "Imagine this. It is Monday morning. I am getting ready to go to work, but my keys are in the refrigerator, my briefcase is at the neighbor's house, my car is at Mr. Brown's house, and my shoes are at the shoe repair shop. Now tell me, what's wrong with this picture?" After a good laugh, your child will reply that disorganization is the problem.

Every night, let your children see you organize your important papers, keys, and other items you need to take to work. Ask your children to make a checklist of all the things they will need for school in the morning. Put homework, lunch money, and other materials in a special place before the children go to bed. Instill organization as a lifetime habit.

Remember, the word *organized* is the main focus here. Don't say, "Amy, come here and put the cap back on the juice bottle." Instead, say, "My, my, Mr. Unorganized seems to have visited us again. He appears to have left the cap off the juice."

Make a checklist for your child on "Things

I would like to do this weekend," and have your child check off his or her favorite activities and do any necessary planning or preparation. Another list to your child may consist of things you would like her or him to help you with this week. The list may include tasks that your child sometimes forgets to perform. Post the list on the refrigerator door or bulletin board and ask your youngster to check off the tasks as they are completed.

Using humor and what-if situations to teach problem solving will also help build your child's creative writing skills. For example, have your youngster pretend that one day, all the workers at the M&M candy factory became disorganized. All the peanut M&M's had coconut inside, and all the plain chocolate M&M's came out grape flavored. Ask your child what would happen to the sales of M&M's if this continued. Encourage her or him to write a short composition titled, "The Day the M&M Workers Became Disorganized."

Many schools today are so busy trying to teach the basics that they have little time to really teach our children to think creatively. And that's where you, the parent, come in.

NOTES

*P*unishment

*Positive punishment is simply a
reinforcement of remembering the
things we should not do.*
                    —Marva Collins

In a world in which so many hands—sometimes the wrong ones—are reaching out to your one, and so many voices are calling, and so many fingers are pointing, it is easy for our children to become confused as to who they are, where they are going, and how they should get there. Misbehavior is inevitable but is a part of every child's learning. *Remember, you, the parent, have the right to choose your response to a child's bad behavior. The way we see the problem can often become the way we approach the solution.* When punishment is necessary, always differentiate the behavior from the child. Let children know that awesome, fantastic, phenomenal children do not behave the way they have just behaved. Say: "I love you very much, all the time, but I am unhappy with your behavior right now. When you are ready to be the bright child that I know you are, we can then talk."

When verbally questioning your child as to why a certain behavior was exhibited, have her or him preface a response with: "I am wonderful, I am fantastic, I am glorious, and I realize that I should not have done that, but I am still growing, I am still learning, and this is what I learned from my behavior, and I conclude that I will not do that again." Here, we are teaching children to accept that they are wonderful and that we still love them, but we want them to understand that their behavior was not desirable, and they must ask themselves: "What did this teach me? What lesson am I to learn from this?"

◆ ◆ ◆ ◆ ◆ ◆ ◆ ◆ ◆ ◆ ◆ ◆ ◆ ◆ ◆ ◆ ◆ ◆ ◆ ◆

TRY THIS
Positive Punishment

After you discuss the misbehavior with your child, have him or her write the letters of the alphabet from A to Z, then write a positive attribute of himself or herself using each letter: I am Adorable, I am Beautiful, I am Courageous, and so forth. This will help reinforce the child's belief in his or her innate goodness.

◆ ◆

NOTES

_____

_____

_____

_____

_____

_____

_____

_____

_____

_____

Reading

Reading makes a ready man.
—Francis Bacon

Growing up as an only child in rural Alabama, I would often ask my mother if I could go to a friend's house to play. She would always retort: "Get a book and read and learn to stay out of other people's houses." I did as she said, and my parents soon began to wonder what kind of bibliophile they had created. I was accused of wanting to do nothing but read. In fact, I bought so many books that I had to hide them from my parents. I would tear the covers of the new books so they would look like they were old.

Books Are a Window on the World

I remember being able to visit Japan, Africa, Switzerland, and other foreign countries through my books. I remember crying, laughing, succeeding, and failing, all because of my identification with some character I had read about in a book. These characters became my solace, my confidants, my villains, my heroes and heroines. They became thought material when sleep escaped me. I learned to fear being motherless when I read "Hansel and Gretel" and "Cinderella." I gained courage when I read "Robert Bruce and the Spider" (see Thinking). I learned never to make excuses and to use time wisely when I read Rudyard Kipling's poem "If." I learned to show kindness to others when I read the poem "The House by the Side of the Road." I learned determination when I read the autobiography of Booker T. Washington. I learned the difference between might and faith when I read the biblical story of David and Goliath. I learned to spell by having my grandmother assign the books of the Bible as a spelling lesson.

Books offer new words, new vocabulary, new ideas, new worlds. Books can teach what parents cannot. Children will seldom argue with what an author writes. When they read the same concepts their parents or teachers have tried to instill in them, they say: "Maybe my parents were right. The author is saying the same thing here in this book." Never pass up the opportunity to explore the morals and themes of the books you read with your children. You can use these lessons to reprimand your children. For example, when a child cannot be easily awakened in the morning, you might say: "Uh-oh! You are not turning into Little Boy Blue on me, are you?" This not only reinforces the lessons you would like your child to remember, but it also enhances your child's ability to recall information.

* *

TRY THIS
Vocabulary Building

Use new words on a consistent basis. For example, all children know the word *big*. Why, then, do we not acquaint them with the words *gargantuan, tremendous, gigantic,* or *huge*? After reading Shakespeare's *Macbeth* with a nine-year-old, I later used the word *death* in a conversation with this youngster. The child said,

"Mrs. Collins, *dead* and *death* are rather ordinary words. Why not say that someone has shuffled off their mortal coil?"

◆ ◆

If children are "immersed" in determination, stick-to-it-iveness, perseverance, kindness, love, hope, loyalty, and a succeeding-against-the-odds, I-can-do-it attitude, they will become great and mighty citizens. Books that teach such values are the ones you should seek out in the library or bookstore. Don't choose books just because they have pretty pictures, cutesy words, and easy-to-read text. Books should be selected to complete the *image* you have for your child.

Many parents never bother to read the books they buy for their children, nor do they preview what their children are reading. We test-drive the cars we buy. We research the quality of the stereo equipment we buy. We have houses inspected before we buy. We need to take the time to research what is in the readers and textbooks our children use in school, and what is in the books we bring home for them. How many parents can truly say, "I know what my children learn and read at school"?

Talk about what you've read in newspapers, magazines, and books. Let your children hear you discuss various issues and ideas. Read the books that your child reads and discuss them with him or her. Ask: "Which character did you like most? Why? Which character did you like least? Why? What did you like most about this book? What did you like least? What did you learn from the book? What vocabulary words did you learn?"

Make an effort to read with your child at least once a week. The philosopher Francis Bacon said: "Some books are to be tasted, some to be swallowed, and some to be digested." Help your child get the most "nutrition" out of the books he or she reads.

NOTES

_____

_____

_____

Self-Reliance

*Believe in your own thoughts,
or you will be forced to hear your own
rejected thoughts spoken by others.*
—Ralph Waldo Emerson

Ralph Waldo Emerson's essay "Self-Reliance" is perhaps the best I have ever read on personal achievement and believing in oneself. Too many youths today are afraid to be the selves they were born to be. Instead, they attempt to join the herd, to be like everybody else.

* *

TRY THIS
A Lesson in Self-Determination

Share the following poem by Edgar Guest with your child.

Myself

I have to live with myself and so
I want to be fit for myself to know.
I don't want to keep on a closet shelf
A lot of secrets about myself
And fool myself as I come and go
Into thinking no one will ever know
The kind of person I really am.
I don't want to dress myself up in a sham.
I want to be self-respecting and
*   conscience free.*
I want to be fit for myself to know.

Just as we are what we eat, we are what we learn. When our schools ceased teaching values, our children then defined and made up their own. Today we have millions of children labeled criminal and any other label we can think of. I call them children devoid of values and a self.

Children with a strong sense of self do not mind being called a nerd or a coward. Being different does not bother them. They know they are different because they have learned to hear the drummer within, and they are not afraid to march to that drummer. They have learned there is nothing wrong with their chosen path in life.

Parents who put their children first will find that their youngsters will always feel comfortable relying on their parents' advice rather than heeding the latest "song" sung by their peers. Peer groups are successful in luring your child only when you, the parent, have not established the unshakable belief that your child is the most important person in your life. When all children can answer the question "What do you know for sure?" by saying, "I know for sure my parents love me, and I know for sure that I am wonderful and unique," we shall see the end of violence, teenage suicide, alcoholism, and all the other ills that beckon our children.

I grew up in a small town in Alabama called Atmore. Racism, lack of jobs, poverty, and every other malady one can think of beckoned me and my sister, Cynthia, but from the day we were born our parents gave us a sense of identity, self, and self-reliance. When my mother saw me off to school each morning, she would call out from the front door, "Don't forget you are a Nettles, and all Nettleses are winners." She never let me forget our family name, and because of all that pride and love, none of the blight and failure surrounding us could ever find a place to fester in our hearts.

NOTES

_____

_____

_____

_____

_____

_____

_____

Thinking

*Thinking is the talking of the soul
with itself.*

—Plato

*D*on't just make up your mind—think!

How many times have we heard, "I wish you would make up your mind"? This, to me, means "just say something. Don't think." Once we teach children the rudiments of good thinking, they will begin the lifetime habit of making good choices, be it in the selection of a toy, in the analyzing of information given, and in their daily behavior.

In order to make up our minds, we should follow all the steps that lead to good thinking. Be a role model to your children by saying: "This is what I think. Do you agree?" Or, "This is what I think. What do you think?" If they are pondering what they wish to do, ask them: "What will be the outcome of this thinking?

What is the worst thing that can happen from this conclusion? What is the best thing that can happen?"

"I disagree," "I agree," and "I think" are all very powerful tools. Encourage children to use them whenever possible. If we don't urge our children to ask questions of themselves and others, they become mere vessels into which we pour information without response.

Never, never say to your child, "Do it because I said so." Just as you are beginning to teach your child to question, you must allow questions from him or her in return. Remember, if your child is allowed to question you, the parent, he or she will also be able to question negative values and conduct in a peer-pressure situation. If we teach our children to accept everything we say at face value, will it not follow that they, too, will slavishly and blindly follow the dictates of their peers?

Young children's beliefs may be scattered and not well honed, but they do have them. The more we allow them to practice verbalizing their beliefs, the more adept they will become in sharpening and focusing these beliefs. It is like a blurred television image: Sometimes we have to work with the buttons to sharpen the reception. We need to work with our children's verbal and analytical buttons in order to sharpen their thinking skills. If we do this consistently, the picture—their vision in life—will become crystal clear.

How often have our children made a certain request or asked us a question, and we reply, "I think…" and go on to espouse our thoughts? Why not ask your child: "What do *you* think?" I remember my own three children requesting gym shoes. My husband and I would then take out the private tuition bills, the utility bills, and the mortgage bills, and spread them out on the table. We would ask them: "What do *you* think? Can we afford the gym shoes? If we buy the gym shoes, we can't pay the mortgage. You will have new gym shoes, but we will not have a house to live in." The children would think and reply: "I think we cannot afford gym shoes." My husband and I would always respond: "Good job! You are so bright and such a wonderful thinker." When children "think it," they reach their own conclusions, not yours.

* *

TRY THIS
Teach Observation

Teach children the creative skill of observing.
For example, while grocery shopping, ask:
"How many people do you think were involved
in the canned-goods section? What was the
process for labeling the cans? Who provided
the printed information for the cans? Who
designed the labels for the cans? What does
nutritional information mean?" You are teaching your child to conceptualize for an intelligi-
ble world.

* *

Avoiding the "Everybody" Trap

"Everybody else is doing it. Why can't I?"
This is a question most children at one time
or another will ask. Say to your child: "How
many children live in this city?" Let your
child know that he or she would need an offi-
cial count to truly say that "everyone" is

doing it. Should the statement be rephrased, "The children I know are doing it"?

"Everybody hates me" is another statement used frequently by the child who has learned to become a "victim." To this question you might respond, "Everybody means everyone in the whole world. This means people in China, Africa, Switzerland, and places you have never visited, so how could these people hate you?" Encourage your child to conclude that not "everybody" hates him or her. Then say, "Let's talk about the people you think hate you right now. Can you think of anything that you may have done to make you feel that these people hate you?"

Once we get our children through all the stages of the analytical process, they will begin to see that things are not always what they seem. In other words, the way we *see* the problem is often the problem.

Thinking involves knowing the significance of perception. If you wear prescription glasses, give them to your children. Ask them to look through the glasses and tell you what they see. They will reply that everything is blurred and unclear. Say, "But I see fine with them. Does this mean something is wrong with you because you do not see what I see when I wear these glasses?" There is nothing wrong with the children's eyes, of course; it just means that the glasses were made for the parent's eyes. Perception, therefore, means that something we see may not necessarily be true. Furthermore, children must learn not to assume that others will perceive things the same way they see them.

♦ ♦

TRY THIS
Nurture Alternative Thinking

When reading bedtime stories, encourage your children to think of other endings to the stories. Have them come up with homonyms and synonyms for certain words and suggest a new beginning for the story. In this manner, we do not program our children to simply accept what others create. Is there little wonder that we repeatedly hear children declare that they committed this or that crime because they saw it on television? Parents are preoccupied with trying to get violence off our television programs, but to me the first priority should be to teach our children to think, to consider all factors, and to determine the strengths and weaknesses of every situation. Once they learn to do this, they will be safe not only from violence on television but also from the negative fingers pointing at and calling to them in the real world. Like the men in the *Odyssey* (see Discipline and Perseverance), they, too, will learn to plug their ears to the violence of our times.

♦ ♦

Forward Thinking and Parallel Thinking

Forward thinking is showing a child an apple and asking, "What is this?" The child looks at us in amazement, as if to say, "It is an apple, of course." *Parallel thinking* goes beyond that. We should encourage the child to say: "It is a red apple [or green or yellow]. Apples grow in this state or that, apples have seeds, apples grow on trees, apples have stems, apples are sweet, apples are sour. There is a story about a man named Johnny Appleseed, who began planting apple seeds in Ohio and spread them across the United States." Here, the child is being taught parallel thinking, to seek alternatives, to ask, "What else can it be?"

I remember when my young daughter planned a birthday party in our garden. I had helped her with the outdoor decorations, and the food was all prepared. A sudden downpour of rain, however, interfered with her plans. I remember her despair when she said: "I am so disgusted. I won't have the party." She was using forward thinking. I said to her, "Why not use the house we just moved from [it was empty at the time, and just around the corner], and then you can still have the party?" We then proceeded to move the food and party goods. She was still able to have the party after all. This is parallel thinking in action.

The Circle of Life

In school, I use an exercise in which I show the students a blank sheet of paper. I ask: "What do you see?" They respond initially, "I see a blank sheet of paper." I soon get them to parallel think so they can say: "I see trees, I see rain, I see the people who fell the trees, I see manufacturing, I see laborers, I see trucks that deliver the paper." They learn that we are all connected. The sheet of paper that we take for granted is the end result of many hands and many activities. We conclude that none of us goes our way alone.

Here are other examples of parallel thinking in action. Say to your child: "Fire is bad, right?" The child will automatically say "Right." But tell them that fire also cooks our food, keeps us warm, and powers certain kinds of machinery. You can do the same thing with water, medicine, cold weather, and so forth to get your youngsters to see that while these things can be bad, they can also be helpful. If your child comes home from school and says, "Danny made a face at me. I hit him, and I got into trouble with the teacher. I was sent to the office," ask your child, "What choices did you have in this encounter? What other choices could you have made?" This kind of conflict resolution allows your children to become steeped in the idea that they are always in control of their behavior and that they always have the power to choose.

* *

TRY THIS
Consider All Factors

Read the story of the Three Little Pigs with your children. Talk to them about alternative materials for the pig who built his house out of straw and for the pig who built his house out of sticks. What are the weaknesses of building with straw and sticks? What other materials might they have used? Why did one pig decide to build his house out of bricks? Was it perhaps because this pig considered all the factors while the other two simply acted without thinking?

* *

A Penny for Your Thoughts

Encourage your children to write down their thoughts and keep them in a Thinking Book. At some point children must be encouraged to act on their thoughts. Parents can repeatedly ask during dinnertime or some other free time, "Any new thoughts today?" A further and repeated question should be: "Have you acted on any of your thoughts?"

If your children become discouraged when a thought does not come to fruition at first, remind them of the two hundred or so tries Thomas Edison went through before he perfected the lightbulb. Children must be taught if at first we do not succeed, we must try, try again. They should be reminded to ask at every junction: "What did I learn from my failure? What are the weaknesses of my project? What are the strengths of my project? What parallel thinking is needed for the success of this project? Did I use only forward thinking?"

One of my favorite stories growing up was that of Robert Bruce and the Spider. Its inspirational take on parallel thinking worked for me. Perhaps it will work for your children, too. The warrior Robert Bruce decided to give up fighting for Scotland because he kept losing the battle he was waging against his adversaries. Lying on a cot in his room one night, he watched a spider try and try again to weave her web. Each time she failed, she tried a new approach. Bruce realized that if the spider can try again and again, he, too, must not give up. He raised himself from his cot and went back out onto the battlefield to win a war he initially thought was impossible. Why? He learned an alternative lesson from a lowly spider. He learned parallel ways of doing something.

NOTES

_____

_____

_____

_____

_____

_____

_____

_____

_____

_____

Uniqueness

*No bird soars too high who flies with
his own wings.*
—Marva Collins

*I am a miracle. I am unique. I am special. There
is not another child like me in the entire world.
There is no one with my eyes, my hair, my nose,
my thoughts, my beliefs, and, of course, not
another child in the world (except my siblings)
has my parents, my brothers, my sisters, and my
grandparents. All this makes me truly unique.*

Teach your child the above declaration at a
very early age, as soon as he or she begins
to talk. Say it to him or her repeatedly. *Many
parents seldom realize that the greatest gift we
can ever give our children is self-determination
and a firm belief in self.* When children value
their uniqueness, they will protect themselves
from drugs, from choosing the wrong friends,
and from self-destruction. They will always

strive to find the self that is truly them rather than connecting to others in an unhealthy way.

A child's "me" is the sum total of what he or she will become. There is the "me" that really exists, the essence of one's self, and there is the "me" that parents think the child is or would like the child to be. Then, there is the "me" that society thinks we are. There is the material "me," the social "me," the evolving "me," the future "me," and the now "me." Getting through to all those "me's" can be a real challenge. Children often develop as many social selves as needed to gain social acceptance.

I remember one student in my second-grade class who stuttered. Whenever he spoke, I would immediately stop everything I was doing and give this child my undivided attention. Soon every other child in the room decided the way to get my attention was to fake a stutter. This is a clear indication of how the young "me" becomes confused as to which "me" she or he should pursue.

Children need to have their uniqueness appreciated. One seven-year-old girl had missed 150 school days out of 195 the year before I became her teacher. One morning she walked into my class wearing her dress inside out. I whispered to her: "Sweetheart, your dress is on the wrong side." She whispered back: "I know, Mrs. Collins, but my dress was dirty on the other side and I did not want to miss school." For the first time in her life, this young child had found a reason to come to school. She felt the "me" inside being given the attention she needed. She felt her self being attended to. She felt comfortable being at school.

♦ ♦

TRY THIS
Who Am I?

When your children are being punished, have them write a set number of answers to the question "Who am I?" The more opportunities children have to think about who they are, the more they will become what they are. The teachers at our schools punish the students when needed by having them write 200 reasons as to why they are too bright to have done this or that. The more children write these affirmations, the more they realize that wonderful people do not do negative things.

♦ ♦

When your child misbehaves, ask: "Which of your 'me's' do you think may have done that?" Encourage your child to say: "The 'me' that did not consider all factors did that." The more you give your children an opportunity to practice being the best "me" they can be, the more they will become grounded in right values and right choices. Most important, they will learn to consider all factors before making a decision. What we are doing is getting children acclimated to thinking: "I will never participate in negativity because I am just too wonderful and too bright."

NOTES

_____

_____

_____

_____

_____

_____

Vocabulary

Without knowing the force of words,
it is impossible to know men.
—Confucius

Most children detest laborious dictionary exercises. To make vocabulary more fun, teach your child a new word each day by using that word in your daily conversation. *I tell children that using the same word each day is like eating the same food for the rest of their lives.*

First, learn to expand your own vocabulary. Make a list of words and definitions from the dictionary. Put this list in a visible place in your home. Memorize one word each day as you go about your daily routine. Then use these words consistently with your children. Leave this list for your babysitter or caregiver so that she or he, too, can use the words.

• • • • • • • • • • • • • • • • • •

TRY THIS
A Whole New Word

Write five notes to your child and place one in his or her book bag each day. These notes not only are positive affirmations of your love for your child, but they teach reading and vocabulary skills. Each note may simply say: "You are an awesome child." "You are phenomenal." "You are laudable." "You are a *belle esprit* (French for "beautiful spirit")." "You are momentous." Use these words in your daily conversations. When your child misbehaves, ask the following question: "Why aren't you going to do that again?" They should be encouraged to respond: "Because I am laudable, I am phenomenal, I am awesome." Learning should never be left in isolation. Repeat and repeat, and one day the recording will come back to you loud and clear. Our children are what we tape.

• • • • • • • • • • • • • • • • • •

NOTES

Winning

Winning is the epitome of honesty itself.
                                        —Marva Collins

In a society in which we are judged by what we have, we often send children the wrong message. We teach them to think that we are only as good as what we last "got."

There is the story of a very rich merchant who always tried to help people in need. A man came to him one day telling of his misery and woe and wants and needs. The rich merchant kept on a shelf a box filled with money for the taking. He said to the man, "Take what you need." The man emptied the entire box. He never returned to repay the debt as he had promised. Two years, three years went by, and finally he mustered enough courage to return to ask for another favor. The rich merchant again said, "Sure, take all you need." The man went to the shelf, only to exclaim: "There is nothing there!" The rich man replied, "Of course there is nothing there. If we take and put nothing back, there will be nothing to take." *How many of our children grow up in a world learning to take and never put back?*

Many poetry books have been written. Many parenting guides have been written. This book will prove to be no different if we simply read it, put it away, and later say: "I once read that book, but I don't remember what it was about." *Remember, if it is not caught, it has not been taught. Therefore, repetition, drill, and daily reminders are the deposits that you, the parent, must make in your child's life-long account.*

♦ ♦ ♦ ♦ ♦ ♦ ♦ ♦ ♦ ♦ ♦ ♦ ♦ ♦ ♦ ♦ ♦ ♦ ♦ ♦

TRY THIS
A Lunchtime Bonus

When you pack a lunch for your child, take the time to put a special note of affirmation now and then into his or her lunch bag. The note will give them something to hang on to in this slippery world. It will also help your child find her or his identity when tempted by peer pressure to join the "crowd." The note might read: "I, [child's name], promise that this day shall be gained, not lost. Today, I shall achieve all that I possibly can, knowing that in the end what I do today will determine my future."

* * * * * * * * * * * * * * * * * * * *

What Is a Winner?

I can't think of a more inspirational way to end than with the following poem, taken from the book *Double Win* by Denis Waitley.

Winning Is What We Give Back

Winning is giving your best self away.
Winning is serving with grace every day.

You'll know that you have won when
your friends say it is true
"I like you, I like who I am when I am
around you.

You look for the best in others you see
And you help us become who we are
*   trying to be."*

Winning is helping someone who's down.
It's sharing a smile instead of a frown.

It's giving your children a hug by the fire,
And sharing the values and dreams
*   that inspire.*
It's giving your parents the message,
*   "I care.*
Thanks, Mom and Dad, for being
*   so fair."*

Winners are willing to give more than
*   they get.*
Their favors are free, you are never
*   in debt.*

Winning is giving one hundred percent.
It's paying your debts, your taxes, and
*   your rent.*
It's trying and doing, not crying and
*   stewing.*

Winners respect every color and creed.
They share and they care for
*   everyone's need.*

*They are always willing to do a
   great deed.*

*The losers keep betting that winning
   is getting,*
*But there's one of God's laws that they
   keep forgetting.*

*And this is the law you can live
   and believe.*
*The more you give, the more you
   will receive.*

Share this poem with your child and post it in his or her bedroom or in the family room. When your child explains that he or she did something because Elizabeth or Timmy did it, you might say: "Are you the kind of winner who makes other people better, or are you the kind of loser who lets other people make you lose?"

When your child repeatedly talks of "wants" and things she or he would like to have, why not quote a line from the poem: " 'Winners are willing to give more than they get.' You are surely a winner, aren't you?"

Again, when children need to be repri-manded, why not let them use what they have learned from the poem? They may write 100 reasons why winners do not lie. After 100 reasons, think what a winner you will have in your child!

NOTES

_____

_____

_____

_____

_____

_____

_____

_____

_____

A Note to Parents on Choosing a School

Our belief systems are our anchor for the decisions we make in every endeavor. If we believe that one food contains more salt than another or more fat than another, we then choose the best alternative. Likewise, to any given situation we must bring with us enough background material to be able to reach rational conclusions. I find it quite interesting as to how parents select schools for their children. Too often the prerequisite is how the school looks. It is essential to find out the *quality* of teaching when choosing a school. Just as we cannot judge a book by its cover, we cannot judge a school by its looks.

Make arrangements to visit the school and observe the classes. If you can, sit in on a class for four or five days. Schedule an appointment with a teacher or administrator to address any questions you may have. Keep in mind the following:

- Are all the children learning, or does the teacher cater only to the brightest achievers?

- Do the children really, really like school? Does the teacher make the learning environment fun and challenging?

- Are all of the children doing the same thing from the same textbook?

- What textbooks are used in the school? Do most of the textbooks contain more pictures than words? Do the lessons involve memory work more than reading work?

- Is seated work busy work, or does it connect to something the child has previously learned?

- Are the children taught perceptually and conceptually?

- Can the children draw analogies?

- Are the children allowed to disagree with a concept given by the teacher?

- Are spelling words assigned, a test given, and five days later the children cannot remember how to spell the words?

- Is there a good logic program at the school?

- Is there a good math program at the school?

- Cognitively, how are the children taught? Scientific evidence indicates that a child whose early cognitive training is neglected will never catch up in intellectual progress to a properly trained child of approximately the same intelligence.

- Are papers corrected immediately? Do the teachers say, "Let's proofread this" instead of "That's wrong, do it over"? To me, the word *proofread* does not leave as negative an effect on children as the words *wrong* and *do over*. If children knew what to do correctly, they would do it in the first place.

- Does the school use a phonics-based program or the look-say, whole-language approach?

- Do the children understand their homework, or does it become the parents' homework? Are the children motivated enough to do more than is asked for in the homework assignment? For example, if there is more than one answer, are the students motivated enough to find them?

- Do the students write daily? Yes, even kindergartners.

- Is there classical literature in the school library? How is the library used? Look through some of the books and see how often they are checked out. Many school libraries are wonderful, but they are not "child-friendly."

- When the children are asked a pointed question, do other children volunteer, "Mrs. Jones, I know something else that is analogous to that," or "Mrs. Jones, I too know another concept or word that means the same"? For example, the students at Westside Prep are not just taught that two plus two equals four. They are taught that forty minus thirty-six will also give us four, and fourteen minus ten will also give us four, and two times two will also give us four. This is called parallel learning.

- Are the children free to make mistakes with a teacher who does not allow ridicule and laughter from the other students? We always tell our students: "If you cannot make a mistake, you cannot make anything. It's okay to make a mistake. This is how we learn." We never allow ridicule and laughter. This ensures every child the freedom to speak his or her thoughts majestically without fear of reprisal.

◆ Do the children do a lot of independent work, or is the teacher constantly interacting with them, mediating errors, and asking probing questions that require children to think, to ponder, to conclude, to add to? Do the children seem to be slaves to their workbooks? I call such children "workbook illiterates." They check a few multiple-choice answers, a few true-or-false answers, and never develop a workable vocabulary.

NOTES

_____

_____

_____

Preparing a Plan for Your Child's Caregiver

If I say to your child, "You are overdrawn," and you say to your child, "You are overdrawn," and siblings and relatives say the same thing, the phrase will soon have meaning. However, if other caregivers say to your child, "You are bad" or some other negative phrase, the child will soon have conflicting values. Take the time to write a brief synopsis for your child's caregiver of what "tapes" you have recorded for your child.

If you have steeped your child in classical music, would you be happy if some babysitter or caregiver came in and played violent, negative tapes for them? We always make sure to leave emergency numbers with our children's caregiver. Why not leave a list of the terms used in your home? Acquaint the caregiver with the words *overdrawn, insufficient funds,* and so forth.

If your caregiver tends to your child on a regular basis, he or she in effect becomes a part of your family. You should familiarize the caregiver with the conduct and values taught and practiced in your home. When the parent or person in charge gives orders to the child, the time is taken to explain why to the child. When telling a child to clean her or his room, have the child repeat, "I promise to clean my room and I am responsible." When the task is not completed, have the child repeat, "I did not clean my room and I am irresponsible." When we allow a child to make excuses for not accomplishing a certain feat or task, we are recording a future tape that says to children that such practices are okay when they are not.

Remember, begin with the end in mind.

Children & Parents Praise Marva Collins & Westside Preparatory School

* *

Shelisa L. Washington
Westside Preparatory Class of 1988

Mrs. Marva Collins is a loving, kind, and gracious lady, who just happens to be the best teacher and educator I have had the great, good fortune to know.... The inspiration I have received from her has enhanced my life. I have only to remember the words of "The Creed" and find renewed strength to keep striving to succeed, for it served as a map on the road of excellence. This spring I graduated from college. My goal is to be as great a teacher as Mrs. Collins.

* *

Talmadge Griffin III

Mrs. Marva N. Collins has taught me to create my own way to self-excellence. I have been taught to filter the important from the irrelevant. I will listen, think, and create so that I may become a leader.

◆ ◆

Mayme Carroll

This marvelous woman, Marva N. Collins, has shown me the paths of excellence and the map on which to draw them.

◆ ◆

Sean Collins

My Grandma is Marva N. Collins. She has taught me many things. From the creed I've learned to work hard and think for myself. She showed me how to plant flowers.

◆ ◆

Dawn Nelson

I have learned that excellence is not an act, but a habit. I know that low aim is truly a sin and that I must not be a conformist. I will follow in the footsteps of those who have come before me, but if I cannot go that way, I will start my own path of excellence. I say we must give up our failing ways to be the achievers we are destined to be. Westside Preparatory School has prepared me for my constant struggle in life's journey.

* *

Parker Fisher

Dear Mrs. Collins:

You taught me excellence at a young age and told me I can be anything I want to if I put my mind to it. I thank you a million times. You taught me that no hill is too high to climb, to take things into my own hands and not to let anyone tell me what I can and can't do, to strive for what I want, to set a goal, and to go for it. I love you for so many reasons. Your body has always been one big heart. You were a principal, friend, and teacher to me.

* *

Mrs. Sandra Nelson

When I became a parent, I wondered where I would send my children to receive an education that would give them the proper tools to accomplish their goals. I wanted my children to go to a school that not only stressed the importance of a strong educational background but strived to give one to the children. Westside Preparatory has truly lived up to my expectations. The teachers at Westside Preparatory School have always expected their students to do the best they could do, not just enough to get by. The staff have always been a moral support to not only the teachers, but the students as well, letting them know that they will always be there to help them through.... My children are now self-motivated, self-generated, and self-propelled to get the most out of the education they are receiving and to always strive for excellence, no matter what path they choose in life.

◆ ◆ ◆ ◆ ◆ ◆ ◆ ◆ ◆ ◆ ◆ ◆ ◆ ◆ ◆ ◆ ◆ ◆ ◆ ◆

Eric T. Collins

"The world is filled with people who do just enough to get by. You must do more than is expected." These words spring from my lips before I can blink. Here I am in 1996 repeating this phrase to my son in the same dining room that once witnessed tense battles between a mother and her nine-year-old son.... I nudge my own son, Sean, to finish his math, and my thoughts drift back to a time when Westside Preparatory School was still a wild notion in the back of my mother's mind. The thought of being average, of not doing everything in your power to be the greatest you could, was a cornerstone of Marva Collins's philosophy....As my thoughts return to the present, I turn to the bright, exuberant little boy next to me. His grimace changes to a smile. And as he decides to give in to my wishes and finish one more worksheet, I grin....Thank you, Mom, for your patience and your wisdom.

* *

Anna Marie Sibley

I love what Westside Preparatory School offers. I feel secure about the education of my daughters. Children attending WSP learn, and the best thing about their learning is that they want to learn and enjoy doing so. Tell me, how can I not appreciate that?

* *

Mrs. Benevers Addy

When my daughter was two and a half years old, I noticed she was having some serious problems, which were confirmed when she attended preschool. My daughter was extremely active and had difficulties in identifying colors, numbers, letters, etc. I had her evaluated and tested at a hospital. I was told that she was hyperactive and there could be a learning disability. My major concern was to help her the best way I could....I called Westside Preparatory School. Mrs. Collins said to me, "Don't let society label your child. Any child who is challenged and encouraged can learn." My daughter was enrolled at Westside Preparatory School at the age of four, and by the age of five she was not only adding and subtracting, she was reading and reciting poems. I feel my daughter would not be the person she is today if she did not receive the quality education she is getting at WSP.

◆ ◆

Cynthia B. Collins

As a young child, I was taught to value education, and I was always told to be the best you can be, no matter what it was. From my mother I was taught that whatever gifts are given to us by God should be shared. As a teacher, I share the love and knowledge that my mother shared with me. I can live forever through the seeds I have planted within my students....Perseverance helps us to understand that a flower can be wilted, but that doesn't mean it can't be revived.

• •

Mrs. Griffin

Putting my children in Westside Preparatory School was one of the best things I could do for them.... Daily the children recite "The Creed." It is a motto that teaches them self-esteem and responsibility.... Westside Preparatory School has also taught my children that education will get you the job, but common sense will keep the job. Westside Preparatory School has provided my children with the smarts needed to survive in the business world as well as providing them with street smarts.

• •

Gwendolyn St. Julian

Marva accepts children as they are and molds them into outstanding students. The students feel as if they can conquer anything. She strengthens and builds their character. Marva Collins is honest. She is up-front. You may not like what she has to say, but when it comes from her I accept it and try to improve. I know she has the best in her heart.... Marva Collins will only say kind words of support. If she can't say anything nice, then she won't say anything at all. She stresses this to the children, which is why they are busy thinking of constructive activities rather than ridicule....An education at WSP is high-power, strenuous, fast-paced, with no time for foolishness. She's known for teaching the classics and morals along with proverbs and Bible scriptures. She practices what she teaches. She works hard....If I had it to do all over again, I would choose Marva Collins again to educate my son. When I gave him Marva Collins, I gave him the world. She gave him the world by sharing her knowledge. She gave him wings to soar at any level he chooses.

♦ ♦ ♦ ♦ ♦ ♦ ♦ ♦ ♦ ♦ ♦ ♦ ♦ ♦ ♦ ♦ ♦ ♦ ♦ ♦

Patrick Collins

Parents are the trees that provide shade to their genetic heirs. Those heirs who are fortunate enough to have parents who give them positive life tapes are indeed rare. I thank my mother for always positively showing me the way. I thank her for disagreeing with me some of the time, but for loving me all of the time....As headmaster of the Marva Collins Preparatory Schools, I have as part of my mission statement the determination to never let the candles of excellence lit by my mother be extinguished.

Teacher

by Marva Nettles Collins

I am in danger, Teacher, you rescue me.
I say things when I am angry,
hurting, or frustrated.
Please forgive me.

I am doubtful and you give me faith.
I am neglected and you make me whole.
I am missing a piece of my total picture
And you help me find the missing pieces;
Teacher, you make me whole.

You, Teacher, ignore the tags, labels,
and the former statistics that stain,
ink-blot and measure me.
When others saw failure, Teacher,
you saw success.
I am a child, and you show me the way.
You know that there is still hope
for me to learn and grow.
You believe that I can be more
than what I am
And you are patient enough to never
give up on me.

You, Teacher, help me to slay
the monsters that
Beckon me to failure. You are my light
in a mind filled
With darkened thoughts.

I have walked around with tapes
that loudly say:
"You are bad…You are a failure…
You are a negative statistic.
Why bother?"
But you, Teacher, always seem to see
the good in me. You work to set
my mind free…
To help me become all that I can be.
When others see the "bad me"
You make me feel so free.
And so, for you, Teacher, I become good.
I am lost, Teacher, and you give
me directions.
I waste time and you show me how to
use time wisely.

You do not nag…you forgive…you
continue to love me unconditionally.
Not just by the nice and consistent
things you say to me, Teacher,
but I see the love for me in your

Eyes and I am shamed
Into being all that I can be.
I, then, dare not let you down.

I am now a success, Teacher.
I did it for you, and before I knew it,
I had become
A success.

You taught me not to see just today,
but the vision of the future.
When I attempt to go backward,
Teacher, you push me forward.
When I tend to be stunted by the failures
of the past, you make me see
the glory of the future.
I, therefore, learn day by day to unblock
my fetid channels of "That's Good
Enough" attitude.
You see each day as my beginning, and
you do not remember
Or remind me of my decadent and
failing past.

When I try to slip back to my
Comfortable past, you reach out
your hand
From the top of your mountain
of excellence

And again, and again, you pull me
To my levels of excellence
And self-determination.
You teach me to want me to learn,
to achieve,
To discover self-reliance.

Because of you, Teacher,
my light of excellence may
At times flicker, but the flame will
Never extinguish, for I hear you,
Teacher, saying, "Reach...reach...come,
I will not let you fail."
Reaching, saying: "You can do it...
You can do it...You can do it..."
And I am motivated
To light the flickering candles
of others remembering
That once you believed in me. You took
A soul thrown and cast away,
and you made me
Believe in me. You made me whole.
You made me free.
Know what? I love you, Teacher.